Stephen Donald Hu

SUPERVISED LEARNING WITH LINEAR REGRESSION

An Executive Review of Hot Technology

CAPITAL IDEATIONS LLC

Published by Capital Ideations LLC
2733 Palermo Ct.
League City, TX 77573

© Monday, September 24, 2018
First Edition Published 2018

ISBN-13: 978-1729266526
ISBN-10: 1729266525

For the Age of Sail; for the Age of Exploration; and for lines of all kinds – such things that connect us all.

TABLE OF CONTENTS

FOREWORD

Foreword

Course Overview

This course provides a detailed executive-level review of contemporary topics in supervised machine learning theory with specific focus on predictive modeling and linear regression. The ideal student is a technology professional with a basic working knowledge of machine learning theory.

Additionally, to better inform the interested student, the final lesson of this course presents samples in Python describing the essential implementation of reviewed regression methods. To reduce space and improve clarity, this code targets a basic Keras environment – this inclusion is not meant as an endorsement of one system over another (all provide benefits); instead, at the time of this writing, Keras simply offers a popular, facile 'frontend' for managing TensorFlow and Microsoft Cognitive Toolkit deep learning systems, all using this popular script.

Course Prerequisites

Although this course presents its subject matter from the perspective of an executive review, the student will benefit from modest experience with a handful of fundamental technical concepts. Specifically, the student will benefit from: a basic understanding of machine learning principles; basic awareness of linear regression methods; and a basic general understanding of information technology principles.

Optional Course Requisites

Also, the interested student will benefit from a basic working knowledge of Python and Keras. Additional working knowledge of one or more of Keras back-end deep learning systems (TensorFlow and Microsoft Cognitive Toolkit will enhance review of included code samples.

Acquirable Primary Skills

Upon completion of this review, the student should acquire improved ability to discriminate, differentiate and conceptualize appropriate implementations of supervised machine learning methods as they relate to regression-based predictive modeling. Additionally, the student should acquire improved general awareness regarding the use of these models as L1-/L2-norm regularizers and loss functions, as well as an improved ability to discriminate between these closely-related application domains.

Acquirable Secondary Skills

Again, the interested student will also benefit from basic, situational awareness regarding the facility with which these regression protocols may be deployed via Keras and Python using TensorFlow and Microsoft Cognitive Toolkit. At the very least, a brief scan of these 'snippets' will help frame and scope the supervised learning development process – a store of knowledge that may be of wider benefit during project management planning and budgeting discussions.

About this Executive Review

This text should serve the student as an 'executive review'; a distillation of essential information without the clutter of formulae, charts, graphs, references and footnotes. Thus, the student will not have a 'textbook' experience (or expense) while reviewing its contents. Instead, the student will quickly pass through a surprising wealth of actionable, easily-digestible technological information without the distraction of extemporaneous considerations.

Naturally, this objective presents a detriment to the truly research-oriented student, however the associated course is not intended to serve fundamental educational needs. Rather, the information contained herein will rapidly and beneficially update the informed professional regarding use of linear regression models as supervised machine learning concepts via review of historical context, state of the art and, with a bit of extra thought, by improving the student's existing capacity for anticipating lucrative trends within the overlying commercial domain. Best of fortunes!

Foreword

COURSE INTRODUCTION

Ordinary Least Squares Linear Regression

About this Introduction

Drawing an analogy from the Cartesian coordinate system, which describes a point in space with three values, this introduction should orient the student within the chaotic space of a new and rapidly advancing technological domain by imparting three levels of insight. The information summarized within this introduction will provide historical background while also describing current state of the art. With these two points of reference in mind, then, the third point of reference, that of the course subject matter, should improve the student's ability to anticipate future trends within this large and vastly influential corpus of technology. Of course, the same information will also prepare the student to derive superior understanding of the subject matter review that follows.

Relevant Nomenclature

To aid the following discussion, several terms first require formal definition. Terms presented in *italicized sans-serif font* may be referenced in the glossary for quick review and definition.

As previously stated, this course focuses on the application of linear regression models to the supervised machine learning process. Regardless of its specific implementation, a *'predictive statistical model'* attempts to quantify the likelihood that a *'latent variable'* (*'hidden parameter'*) will produce the predicted value, given the value of an *'observable variable'* (or *''visible parameter'*). Besides the obvious challenges related to model development, this process of model-building inevitably devolves to discussions regarding *'risk'*, *'noise'*, *'error'* and the like. These concepts represent potentially confounding affects attributable to the dataset (or its utilization).

Occasionally, these elements of 'noise' are, in fact, other data of limited interest to the current solution. More typically, noisy data represent random errors of some kind and, as such, offer nothing definitive to any solution developed from analysis of the underlying dataset. Consequently, efficacious statistical models typically include some method for managing this interference.

Within the context of this discussion, '*error*' is not the same thing as a '*mistake*'. Rather, the error discussed here represents often unavoidable '*variation*' in the system – whether at the point of measurement/observation or as a natural attribute of the system of interest. '*Observational error*' ('*experimental error*'), refers to variance within observational/experimental equipment, which typically relates to operational limitations. In turn, observational error consists of '*systematic error*' and '*random variation*' – that is, fluctuations due to equipment or personnel, as opposed to fluctuations within the observational system. This, then, presents another perspective on the concept of 'error'.

The concept of '*precision*' describes error of self-relatedness, while '*accuracy*' describes errors of true-value. Because it serves as a quintessential example, imagine a traditional practice target with a cross-hairs and bull's eye fixed at the center of its circular face. Each concentric ring of alternating red-on-white might represent something meaningful – a score gradient or a simple area-based method of ascribing an 'error' measurement to the crosshairs. After twenty arrow-flights, a pattern may emerge.

Where this pattern makes a tight collection of arrows – *i.e.*, all of the arrows land within a squared centimeter of space – then the flight of arrows demonstrates 'precision' (itself a relative term – more on this in a few words). Of course, this result could represent a mere fluke – only repetition will demonstrate empirical evidence that confirms the arrows are, indeed, falling so closely together due to some real, but perhaps unknown, influence. When this pattern repeats itself, however, evidence mounts to indicate a definite '*relationship*' within the pattern.

Extending this example, consider the crosshairs of the target space – this is the *true* objective of the arrow flights. This is also the experiment's primary measure of *accuracy*. No matter how precise the arrow flights might be, the final goal of the demonstration should be their deposition at (or near) the intersection of these two fine lines. Where the flights group close together with precision, but fail to cluster about the true target, then these attempts succumb to errors of accuracy. In other words, a given sample of arrows might land with exquisite precision yet embarrassing accuracy. The converse is also true, and this form of error can be most confusing of all.

When a flight of arrows lands almost randomly about the target space, but somehow manages to center, or focus, its landings around the crosshairs, then its outcome demonstrates accuracy in absence of precision. No matter how scattered the results may be, an assessment of average performance may produce an uncanny lack of 'accuracy error', though the same pattern may seem diffuse to the point of randomness. Given a single attempt, no rational judge could look at such a widespread pattern and argue for actual intent on the part of the competitor.

Then again, if the same competitor staged a similar performance ten, one-hundred or, better, one-thousand times, then the lack of precision starts to look more like true accuracy. Perhaps, given this scenario, we find that the competitor is standing on a hilltop five hundred meters from the target, a feat that would unquestionably suggest competitive skill (while arguing against random effect). Thus, both accuracy and precision are qualified, often subjective, estimates of error. *E.g.*, a judge may tolerate more error in a long-range contest, given the subsequent introduction of additional challenges to performance due to increased range-to-target.

Incidentally, another term for error of precision is called '*bias*'. Likewise, another term for error of accuracy is called '*variance*'. These topics appear repeatedly within the text that follows

Another common set of concepts, which the student will encounter in a professional domain – often to the production of some confusion – are the terms '*loss function*' and '*regularizer*' (there are many others, as you will see in the Keras code samples, but these two are the most common and, so, serve as adequate stand-ins for their kindred). Summarily defined for now, a loss function is, in simplest terms, a method for applying a '*penalty*' to the nodes of a graph model (or the parameters of a linear model) during '*training*' ('*supervised learning*' or '*unsupervised learning*'). The nature of the loss function will determine how well the model represents existing data and how well it generalizes, or adapts, to new data. Closely related, a '*regularizer*' is another function implemented to reduce error within a model (either of bias or of variance, or both). Many of the models described within this course also apply as loss functions and/or regularizers.

These varied levels of application of the same concept begin to present to the novice user as a '*fractal*', which is a pattern that repeats at all levels of interest to present the same (or very similar) pattern. An example might be the vesicular nature of a forest, branching up from stem, to limbs, to branches, to twigs and, then perhaps deeper, into the various cellular structures, which are often also 'tree-like', *etc...*

Resist this source of confusion. Within the context of this course, the model, itself, provides focus. Once the student better understands their applicability, functionality and limitations, then applying them as L1/L2 loss functions or regularizers (or any similar variant) should become a more clear-cut endeavor. Have no worries, however, because this text reviews L1/L2 concepts with greater detail in the passages that follow.

Next, the concepts of '*robustness*' and '*stability*', as applied to the application of linear regression models, also requires a bit of clarity in foreword. A 'robust' model is one that tolerates error better than a model said to be 'less robust' (whatever that might entail). For example, a linear method that employs a means for quantifying and adjusting to data distributions according to a '*least absolute deviation*' (*LAD*) is more robust than a model that uses '*least squares*' (*LS*), since the former is more tolerant of outliers. Thus, where these outlying data points can or should be ignored, then the former approach may serve best (this approach is also a form of the L1-norm, while the latter approach is a form of the L2-norm – more on this later).

LAD methods find applications in many areas, due to their robustness compared to LS. The LAD method is robust in that it is resistant to outliers in the dataset. This may be helpful in studies where outliers may be safely and effectively ignored. If it is important to pay attention to any and all outliers, then LS methods may present a better choice.

Conversely, stability demonstrates the opposite effect. In the previous example, LS methods are more stable than LAD methods, since the former model will not much change with the addition of new data, while LAD may produce wildly variant regressions in the same scenario. In part, this behavior results from the fact that LAD (L1) methods present many possible solutions within the dataset, while LS (L2) methods have a single unique solution (see L1/L2 discussion, below).

Finally, an 'underdetermined system' is one that has more data features than parameters (or more observable values than functional variables). Conversely, an 'overdetermined system' is one that presents more parameters than data features. Models of the former system will tend to 'underfit' the solution, while models of the latter system will tend to 'overfit' the solution.

These terms make regular appearances in the discussions that follow. For now, the student should recognize them, understand them on a basic level and prepare to refine these concepts as the course progresses.

Course Overview

Within the context of this coursework, all the many and vast endeavors in statistical science render to two rough collections of concepts. The first crude order contains all *'traditional'* (*'hard-coded'* or *'rule-based'*) algorithmic models – including many applications that employ the models described within this course. The second order contains everything else – here meaning, primarily, graph-based non-parametric models (*'machine learning'* models). The differences between these concepts can be both subtle and profound.

Primarily, however, the differences between these models generally devolves to discussions of development. Traditional methods of analysis, as applied to large, complex datasets (though not the *"big data"* sets of modern consideration) proceeds in a complex and manually-invented way. In other words, multiple scientists and engineers might expend a great deal of collective effort while analyzing a complex dataset to create a series of rules that adequately model performance of the underlying system.

For example, simple linear regression provides a simple model for simple systems, because the hidden parameters (*'features'*) of linear systems vary in a straight line according to the value of observed variables. The discovery of these 'data features' as a process is called *'feature engineering'*. Most natural systems of interest are not simple enough to be amenable to application of linear models. Thus, more complex problems require evermore complex solutions.

For example, application of these methods to analysis of the English language, word-part by word-part, requires countless rules and exceptions – rules within rules and exceptions within exceptions. In short, the application of 'rule-based' or 'hard-coded' models to such a complex, chaotic system quickly becomes intractable.

This is where graph models and machine learning shine. Rule-based models often require a great deal of manual effort during development, although they tend to run efficiently within computational space, once deployed. Graph models and the '*artificial intelligence*' they support, automatically 'learn' features within the dataset, so they both develop *and* execute efficiently. At least, this is the ideal.

Training these models, then, becomes an exercise of increasing efficiencies. This marks the fractal junctures hidden within the overlying corpus of technology. The linear (and not-so-linear) regression models reviewed herein 1) exemplify the simplest statistical methods capable of demonstrating (and benefiting from) machine learning and 2) these same models often serve to refine deep learning component models, as well – and in various ways!

Again, the focused student will resist confusion. She must first understand these statistical concepts as models, themselves, before attempting to explore their implications as L1/L2 tools. Of course, these concepts are closely entwined, so one cannot exist (or be subjected to discussion) entirely within a vacuum.

In conclusion, regarding nomenclature, the focus of this coursework is supervised learning with linear regression. Next, a word about machine learning seems appropriate.

Machine Learning, Four Broad Application Domains

Broadly speaking, machine learning applications tend to fall into four large problem domains, *'classification'*, *'clustering'*, *'dimensionality reduction'*, and *'prediction'*. Given the nature and computational demands of machine learning applications, the underlying datasets tend to be large (and, oftentimes, sparse, of both data and features), which is the domain of machine-learning-driven analysis.

Classification models analyze these 'big data' sets to provide a means for categorical prediction using *'labeled data'*. Clustering is a similar operation that performs categorical prediction using *'unlabeled data'*. Dimensionality reduction is an exploratory effort directed at identifying and eliminating uninteresting (or confounding) features within the dataset. Finally, predictive modeling, or regression, attempts to analyze the data to support some method for predicting its future performance. Along with the principles of supervised machine learning, this last problem domain, predictive modeling with regression, provides the core subject matter of this course.

Course Focus – Managing the Fractal

As previously stated, the following text cannot help but touch upon the ubiquitous machine learning concepts of L1-/L2-labeled phenomena. Essentially, the models described within this course often appear as L1-/L2-norm loss functions, regularizers, constraints and more – all of these being central concepts related to machine learning. For now, the diligent student will focus on understanding the described regressions first as stand-alone models.

Identifying their relationships with L1/L2 operations will become easier as the discussion progresses.

Overview (Supervised Machine Learning)

While these concepts appear to be a bit more complicated within more advanced graphical models, the essential nature and intent of their application will not change dramatically from one implementation to another. Thus, an attempt to begin at the beginning – that is to say, from the perspective of simple linear regression – will provide key insights into more advanced related topics.

In fact, every statistical model represents an attempt to pry signal from noise by accommodating various sources of error attributable to both the system and observation of it. As previously stated, within the realm of machine learning, the regressions described below apply at multiple levels, especially as regards to their deployment as L1-/L2-norms. Again, however, this course describes them as models, in their own right, while discussing the many ways in which their various configurations interact with machine learning theory to perform loss function and regularization services (among others).

Generalization Error (The Variance/Bias Tradeoff)

Taken together, the two broad categories of error typically encountered with statistical analyses, bias and variance, represent a larger pool of error called '*generalization error*'. Remember, the goal of a statistical model is to provide an analysis that is both precise *and* accurate, although precision and accuracy both have desirable characteristics that can occasionally be the primary focus of model development, as well. Whichever the case may be, optimal model performance requires optimal management of error – and not always with an equal treatment. Sometimes, model developers trade bias for variance and *vice versa*, all depending upon focus of the model and its objective purpose.

Unfortunately, these concepts are not mutually reducible. Often, interactions intended to minimize/maximize the effects of one necessarily produces an opposite effect against the other. In this way, generalization error expresses the '*bias/variance tradeoff*' or the '*variance/bias tradeoff*', again, depending upon perspective.

These features of the model often come under control of the developer's choice of loss-function or regularizer. Those words again! Once the student understands how these comparatively simple regression models work, then understanding of their deployment as L1/L2 affecters will seem infinitely more reasonable.

Because this bias/variance tradeoff plays such an important role in model design – especially as relates to selection of L1/L2 operators – a brief but slightly more detailed review of these errors will benefit the student. This deliberate repetition should 1) reinforce their importance within the machine learning domain and 2) ensure the firm acquisition of these concepts on the part of the student.

Within the following passages, please note use of the term 'training data' here, since the model is no longer in development mode when engaged in testing and/or evaluation. This means it can no longer change to adapt to any new features it might encounter within the dataset – it can only perform well or poorly, depending upon efficacy of its design.

Variance Error

Loosely stated, variance error is a measure of the model's sensitivity to small fluctuations in training data. Another way to perceive variance error is via the perspective of supervised learning. The 'supervised' nature of this process intends to 'teach' the model to 'discriminate' (for predictive models – classification models will 'classify'). This ability of discrimination is as much a measure of the model's ability to provide one output over another, as it is a measure of the model's ability to distinguish signal from noise, regardless of its origins. When a model demonstrates variance, this often implies a failure of training, wherein the model has inadvertently, and incorrectly, learned to model the noise as though it were signal. This, of course, is a useless outcome that can only degrade the model's performance.

Variance is always a failure of generalization. This means the model cannot readily adapt to the new data introduced to it after training time.

Oftentimes, variance arises due to an excessively complex model – one that analyzes dataset features using too many parameters. Since model behavior inherently attempts to apply some real meaning to all its parameters, these models will tend to '*overfit*' the training data. This is, essentially, the model's attempt to ascribe meaning to parameters where such meaning is, in reality, nonexistent – in fact, this 'meaning' is really 'noise', which will then pass through training to testing/evaluation (and, if not caught, deployment) as bogus predictive capacity called 'bias error'.

If a real data trend is a somewhat 'wavy' line, and a 'good' working model will produce a line that is, more or less, almost as 'wavy' – not significantly more and not significantly less – then an '*overfitted*' or '*variance-prone*' model will present an even 'wavier' predictive line – one that wanders excessively 'in' and 'out' of the system's true performance space. In a sense, the model 'sees more variation than is actually present within the underlying dataset'. Thus, its predictions will vary where they should not while attempting to replicate noise that it 'perceives' as signal (which the model can never do, since the noise is simply randomness that cannot, by definition, be described by any practical model).

Bias Error

Loosely stated, bias error is attributable to erroneous assumptions within the model. This is a measure of the difference between the model's parameter values as compared to the system's true parameter values (or, in the case of an over-simplified model, one that contains fewer parameters than are necessary to adequately fit the data). Another way to perceive bias error is via the perspective of supervised learning. The 'supervised' nature of this process intends to 'teach' the model to 'discriminate' (for predictive models – classification models will 'classify'). This ability of discrimination is as much a measure of the model's ability to identify one hidden parameter over another, as it is a measure of the model's ability to ascribe appropriate values to those parameters. When a model demonstrates bias, this often implies a failure of training, wherein the model has inadvertently, and incorrectly, placed more (or less) than justified emphasis (weight) to a model parameter (or parameters). This, of course, produces a useless outcome that can only degrade the model's performance.

Like variance, bias is always a failure of generalization. This means the model cannot readily adapt to the new data introduced to it after training time.

Oftentimes, bias arises due to an excessively simple model – one that analyzes dataset features using too few parameters. Since model behavior inherently attempts to apply some real meaning to all its parameters, these models will tend to *'underfit'* the training data. This is, essentially, the model's attempt to ascribe a simple (or null) meaning (value) to parameters where such meaning is, in reality, more complex or nonexistent (alternately, this is an attempt to erroneously 'condense' the signal attributable to multiple *real* parameters as applied to fewer *model* parameters). In fact, this 'meaning' is, again, really 'noise', which will then pass through the model as bogus predictive capacity called 'bias error'.

Using the same metaphor as before, if a real data trend is a somewhat 'wavy' line, and a 'good' working model will produce a line that is, more or less, almost as 'wavy' – not significantly more and not significantly less – then an 'underfit' or *'bias-prone'* model will present an even 'flatter' predictive line – one that runs smoothly where it should wander 'in' and 'out' of the system's true performance line. In a sense, the model is biased for one or more *'real parameters'* or, worse, it is biased for one or more *'false parameters'*. Thus, its predictions will vary inappropriately in an attempt to replicate noise that it 'perceives' as signal (which the model can never do, since the noise is simply randomness that cannot, by definition, be described by any practical model).

Loss Function

Real data are noisy data. Otherwise, we would not need models. In this regard, model designers have a choice. They can choose to manually develop specific rule-based methods for deriving a given model – a tedious and time/expense consuming endeavor called '*manual feature engineering*'. Conversely, the developer can employ a '*machine learning*' technique to force the model to teach itself how to emulate the underlying reality. By definition, this learning process requires some form of feedback to produce viable results.

Machine learning comes in two 'flavors'. '*Supervised learning*' and '*unsupervised learning*' are, as their labels imply, fairly self-explanatory concepts – at a glance. This course focuses on 'supervised learning' techniques – due to densities of subject matter, the student must complete another course to master 'unsupervised learning' concepts.

Further implied by the label, supervised learning requires some means of supervision. In the traditional, rule-based paradigm, this supervision is entirely manual – human-based. Within supervised learning, this process is automated, often by the attributes of a selected model, itself.

Simply speaking, then, a '*loss function*' is a method for evaluating the performance of statistical models. Deep Learning (DL) models rely on loss functions to optimize performance while reducing errors attributable to bias and/or variance. Typically, a loss function works during training to iteratively select and refine optimal parameters (and parameter values) that reflect performance of the true system.

Once the model completes training against the target dataset, a round of '*cross-validation*' quantifies its abilities against a related but previously unseen '*testing/evaluation dataset*'. This terminal measure of the loss function, then, describes the production model's capacity for realistic prediction (or classification), thus quantifying its practical, deployable utility.

These loss functions need not be complex constructs. In fact, the simplest form of machine learning, '*Ordinary Least Squares Regression*' (*OLS* or *OLSR*) uses an exceedingly simple loss function to refine its parameter estimates. This '*learning supervisor*' is simply its iterative calculation of the model's '*Mean Squared Error*' (*MSE*). Each round of calculation subtly (or dramatically, as the case may be) alters the model's layout to refine (learn) its predictive regression line – thus supervising the model's learning experience.

Depending upon the nature of its operability, loss functions are primarily categorized as being associated with the '*L1-norm*' or '*L2-norm*'. More on this in a moment.

Regularizer

Similar to the loss function, a regularizer is a method for resolving '*ill-posed*' problems to avoid overfitting. A mathematical model of a natural phenomenon is '*well-posed*' when 1) a solution exists, 2) the solution is unique, and 3)
the solution's behavior changes continuously with the initial conditions. Conversely, then, an ill-posed problem is one that fails to present one or more of these conditions – as most natural phenomena of modern interest tend to do.

When these '*model assumptions*' fail, regularization may overcome the resultant limitations. Simply stated, a regularizer is simply a function that introduces additional information to the problem, thereby facilitating a new method of sampling from the underlying dataset. Again, this process is not a core subject matter of this text, however several of the regressions described below use the same concepts during implementation, so a brief discussion of these protocols will be of no small assistance to the interested student.

Leaving the detail for passages to come, for now keep in mind that the information added to the problem primarily represents a term called '*lambda*'. This is also called the '*shrinkage coefficient*' or '*ridge factor*' and it is essentially an iterative refinement of '*weights*' or '*weight factors*' applied to a model's hidden parameters to increase or decrease their individual (and combined) contribution to the model's overall performance. This process reduces bias within the model output without significantly altering its variance.

Depending upon the nature of its operability, like loss functions, regularizers are primarily categorized as being associated with the '*L1-norm*' or the '*L2-norm*'. The student will benefit from a brief description of these concepts, which follows.

L0 vs. L1 vs. L2

While not truly a form of 'norm', the student may first wonder why *L0-norm* is never an object of discussion. In fact, L0-norm, or its pseudo-representation, offers many intriguing possibilities to the theoretical mathematician – unfortunately, these same challenges are computationally daunting as well. So, 'L0' and 'L0-norm' are not in practical use at the time of this writing. Nevertheless, this section starts here.

All forms of the norm apply at multiple levels, as previously described, including the theoretical norm L0. While not a true norm, since it is instead a 'cardinality', or collection of non-zero numbers. L0 does occasional make an appearance as a '*vector*' of non-zero values. Essentially, the L0-norm is a simple '*count*' of non-zero elements contained in a one-dimensional array.

To be a true norm, L0 would have to be a 'vector'. A vector is 'two numbers in one', in that it contains a '*cardinality*' (or '*magnitude*') and a '*direction*' – both of which are numbers. Combined together, all the non-zero elements of a whatever (a model, for example), transform into a kind of vector, though this is the same one-dimensional array previously described (not a true vector).

In contrast, L1 represents a '*Manhattan distance*' or '*taxicab distance*' based on summation of absolute values ('*distances*') – again, of the vectors contained within a whatever (a model). L2 represents the familiar Euclidean distance, which derives from a summation of the square root error described by the vector's values (distances). This, then, is the primary difference between L1 and L2 concepts – the former represents a summation of absolute values while the latter represents a summation of squared values. Both are estimates of error.

That's it! Well, a bit more follows, actually, but this really is the essence of the thing. The reason for this will become clear as coursework proceeds.

Again, because this subject matter cannot avoid it or exist in a vacuum without it, the student will benefit from a preliminary evaluation of L1 as compared to L2 benefits. For now, review these points of order, but keep in mind the underlying simplicity of the ideal. "Summation of absolutes *versus* summation of squares".

L0

As a loss function, L0 presents interesting opportunities related to the analysis of sparse solutions to an '*underdetermined system*'. This is a current focus of active research. Unfortunately, as a regularizer, the L0-norm (or its pseudo) currently lacks a mathematical representation – this means that computational solutions do not exist. In fact, for those in the know, this is an NP-hard problem (for the rest of us, the term 'NP-hard' means 'practically impossible'). This is why the student will not soon see much of L0.

L1

Often referred to as '*Least Absolute Deviations*' (*LAD*) or '*Least Absolute Errors*' (*LAE*) '*Least Absolute Value*' (*LAV*), '*Least Absolute Residual*' (*LAR*) or '*Sum of Absolute Deviations*' (*SAD*), the L1 norm condition often serves as both (or either) loss function and regularizer. As a loss function, L1 is robust but unstable, since it presents multiple possible solutions. As a regularizer, L1 works well to produce sparse models, but quickly becomes computationally prohibitive as data/feature density increases. A primary benefit of L1 regularization is its applicability to selectively reduce some coefficient weights to zero – thus removing unnecessary parameters from the final model.

Clearly, this is an automated form of model simplification and '*variable selection*'. Recall these models all include a means of '*data fitting*' during model construction, and further recall that their original applications (Least Squares, perhaps) initially worked to reduce bias without significantly affecting variance (as compared to a simple linear regression, which provides no means of learning – or '*error correction*'). This L1 (and L2) capacity represents its primary utility as a model, a loss function, a regularizer and the like, depending on model design criteria.

L2

Often referred to as '*Least Squares Error*' (*LSE*), as a loss function, the L2-norm condition is not robust, but it is stable, since its operational affect 'guarantees' one solution. As a regularizer, L2 is computationally efficient, due to availability of analytical solutions, but it provides non-sparse output. *I.e.*, its squares-based effect only drives parameter weights (values) *toward* zero – in contrast, the summation-based effect of L1 *forces* some parameter weights to zero, hence its benefit as a variable selector. L2 provides no capacity to simplify model structure, since it provides no means of variable selection.

Course Focus – Revisiting the Fractal

By now, the repeated return to L1/L2-labeled concepts within a discussion of various linear regression methods should begin to make sense to the diligent student. These concepts are, essentially, a way of describing functions that support the supervised machine learning process. No small wonder that these same tools should also be useful as standalone models, too. This is 'where it all began', in a manner of thinking. This also the focus of the current course.

The passages that follow provide a relatively detailed review of Ordinary Least Squares, Ridge, Lasso, Elastic Net and non-parametric regression methods. All serve as increasingly capable examples of supervised machine learning algorithms. These functions also make regular appearances as L1-/L2-norm loss functions, regularizers, and more. By course conclusion, all will be clear. Or, at least, within a margin of error, all will be *clear enough*.

Lesson Conclusion and Course Preview

While the introduction makes repeated references to simple linear regression, the following discussion begins with a review of Ordinary Least Squares Regression (OLS or OLSR). The difference between these methods is, as usual, both subtle and profound – the former is strictly a manual undertaking, while OLSR provides a basic means of automated, supervised machine learning.

OLS methods capably produce viable models, but these approaches often fail when applied to large, naturally chaotic datasets. Primarily, OLSR lacks a means for model simplification.   Ridge Regression presents an L2-norm approach to supervised learning by providing a means for weighting the model's parameters to adapt to ill-posed problems.   While this method provides a method for properly weighting its parameters, a form of '*parameter optimization*', it is not a '*sparse solution*'. More on this later.

Due to increased computational demands, L1-norm approaches to supervised machine learning may currently seem less common, as compared to L2-norm methods, but these protocols offer distinct advantages to the applicable design.   Primarily, Lasso regression, our L1-norm exemplar, provides a means for variable selection according to the way it manages risk (or error).

As the eager student might expect, designers also combine the effects of L1-norm and L2-norm methods by employing Elastic Net Regression. This iterative supervised learning routine performs a Ridge Regression operation followed by Lasso regularization, each weighted according to an adjustable coefficient within the algorithm.

Where L1/L2 methods lack the necessary response, non-parametric and kernel-based protocols become considerations for review. Primarily, this section of the course focuses on the use of Support Vector Machines as Kernel Machines.

Finally, machine learning is currently providing effective solutions within a wide variety of academic, commercial and industrial settings. Due to its statistical nature, *supervised* machine learning methods will most commonly appeal to statisticians tasked with analyzing large, chaotic, real-world datasets. Indeed, these datasets are the focus of exploding global interest, since many of them are just now coming into range of modern theoretical capabilities and leading-edge computational capacities.

Ordinary Least Squares Linear Regression

ORDINARY LEAST SQUARES LINEAR REGRESSION

Ordinary Least Squares Linear Regression

Lesson Overview

'*Ordinary Least Squares Regression*' (*OLSR* or *OLS*) is, by some perspective, the simplest supervised machine learning algorithm. Its ability to learn *and* to supervise that learning is directly attributable to the way it manages error within the regression. In contrast, a '*simple linear regression*' makes no attempt to accommodate error within the model – rather, this method only *reports* (describes/quantifies) error with its prediction. This is, of course, its primary benefit compared to methods that provide no means of describing the '*certainty*' of their predictive value (the opposite condition to '*error*'), but statisticians oftentimes require greater control over potential sources of noise.

Alternately, the designer oftentimes cannot apply such a simple model, at all, given its excessive '*assumptions*'. Recall, these are constraints or conditions that restrict application of a particular method according to the nature of the analytical dataset (or the system deriving it). For example, a simple linear regression requires: 1) weak '*exogeneity*' – or a lack of error in the predictor variables; 2) '*linearity*' – the underlying system should vary in a line-like fashion according to the value of predictor variables; 3) '*homoscedasticity*' – observational values demonstrate consistent error, these values do not change over time or conditions; 4) '*independence*' – observational error demonstrates no variable-to-variable relationships; and 5) lack of '*multicollinearity*' – this is a common point of failure as regards application of simple regression to large natural datasets, since it requires that none of the predictor variables demonstrate relationships, either. Obviously, with rare exception, few systems are amenable to such analysis without a great deal of care and feeding during application.

Inevitably, these assumptions fail, rendering simple linear models invalid. Specifically, where the assumption of homoscedasticity and/or non-multicollinearity fails, the designer next moves to alternate models, and this is oftentimes a variation of Ordinary Least Squares, which minimizes loss without penalizing model complexity, thus providing a form of '*Empirical Risk Minimization*'.

Like all methods, OLSR also presents shortcomings. While it offers a simple error-based means for data-fitting, least-squares provides no method for '*regularization*'. This is the subject matter of following chapters.

Relevant Nomenclature

By now, the attentive student might be mulling a few new, impressive words. Chief among them, '*homoscedasticity*' and '*heteroscedasticity*' are statements of dependence/independence among variable errors. A system is *homoscedastic* when variance in its performance varies consistently. An example of heteroscedasticity, by comparison, might include the description of a production machine that gradually degrades such that its precision decreases in correlation to the length of its service. From a temporal perspective, the machine's error will seem variable, since its '*magnitude*' (raw value) will increase over time.

The fantastical term '*multicollinearity*' presents another whopper. Multicollinearity is a nested measure of predictability. A simple statistical model will exploit the relationship of observational and predictive variables to make some statement about the underlying system. Thus, the model is predictive. Multicollinearity arises when the predictor variables, themselves, are predictable by one another. *I.e.*, one or more predictor variables are

significantly related, such that one varies consistently with
another. Imagine the dual effect of these predictors on the
outcome of the model – if the designer attempts to
manipulate them as independent operators, the system will
not perform according to expectations. These systems will
benefit from OLS regression.

An '*overdetermined system*' is one that presents more
variables than parameters. Here, the term 'parameters'
refers to the predictive variables of the previous passage,
while the term 'variables' refers to observational values.
When a system presents more parameters than variables, it
is '*underdetermined*'. Overdetermined systems oftentimes
derive confused and *variant* models, since the model's
internal functionality will attempt to ascribe non-existent
meaning to its profusion of parameter values. Thus,
overdetermined systems are prone to derivation of '*overfit*'
models – models that have learned to represent '*noise*' as
'*signal*' (which they can never really do, since noise is
inherently meaningless). In the same way,
underdetermined systems also tend to derive confused and
biased models, since the model's internal functionality will
make erroneous assumptions about the underlying system,
given a lack of parameters sufficient for describing its
variation. Thus, underdetermined systems are prone to
derivation of '*underfit*' models – models that have
mistakenly emphasized and/or deemphasized the vital input
of true hidden variables within the system.

Finally, a word on supervised learning. Typically, this is
an iterative process within an iterative process – sometimes
nested several levels deep. At a minimum, a model
designer will generally divide her target dataset into
portions.

The first portion will provide training input.   Because course focus is *supervised* machine learning, these will be *labeled* input.   This labeling, in coordination with the designer's   choice   of   architecture,   loss   function, regularizers,   and   etc...,   provides   a   ready   means   for supervising adjustment of model parameters to improve predictive performance.   When training completes, the second portion of the original dataset supports an intensive round of testing and evaluation.   This process quantifies expected performance of the trained model, since it must (ideally) adapt to new data points, which were not included in   the   training   set.   Again,   the   labeled   data   support assessment   of   error   during   this   round   of   model development, and this error, in turn, describes the model's capacity for generalization, previously described.

OLSR   is   a   ubiquitous   topic   within   these   related discussions.   According to its placement at the root of the story, this discussion of the method begins at the beginning.

Historical Context

In   many   ways,   the   Age   of   Sail   –   that   is,   the   Age   of Exploration   –   is also the developmental source for many foundational concepts that ultimately produced something like OLSR.   Over time, as these intrepid explorers sailed – and sometimes *sank* – around the globe, the navigators of each voyage continuously compiled logs of their travels, to include   countless   references   to   celestial   sightings,   which they used to fix a point on the globe.   As these ship's logs returned to archive, diligent cartographers and astronomers worked together to compare all these sightings according to date,   time   and   geographical   coordinates.   Eventually,   an astronavigational 'picture' developed – albeit a fuzzy one.

Naturally, given the enormous associated risk, each navigator must make a best attempt honest and accurate measurements, yet these way-markers rarely aligned! Given an abundance of choices, then, someone tasked with preparing an updated edition of nautical charts must make choice: which measure is the *best* measure? This single question immediately leads to many others (which might first produce a formal definition of the term 'best'). Someone likely suggested the average value, since this seems an obvious first choice, but this probably didn't help much with especially troublesome entries – those with excessive variations (imagine trying to 'shoot the sun' while cresting ten-meter waves in gale-force winds howling amid Antarctic seas). Thus, a chart entry might provide an *estimated* value (whatever this might be), along with an *estimation of its error.*

These concerns induced considerable theoretical and practical work directed at refining this process, eventually delivering many ideations of general benefit to the study of statistics. As relevant examples, the '*Method of Averages*' (an 18th Century method for analyzing overdetermined systems of equations) and the '*Method of Least Absolute Deviation*' (a slightly more efficient calculation similar to OLS), are *manual* (as in quill and ink) methods for further exploiting the inescapable nature of 'error' to minimize its introduction into model design without attempting to eliminate it (a manner of 'embracing the horror', since these experiences reveal how variable the 'real world' can be). In fact, using statistical protocols like these, systems of both measurement and tabulation improved to the point that astronomers could begin to share their heavenly perspectives in a much more quantified and mathematically rigorous way.

Overview (Ordinary Least Squares)

First and foremost, the 'Ordinary Least Squares Regression' (OLS or OLSR) method is a form of linear regression. Additionally, the 'least squares' aspect of the calculation provides an iterative means of 'data fitting', which is simply any attempt at making rational adjustments to a model with the goal of reducing error (conversely improving precision and accuracy). OLSR oftentimes provides a best approximate solution of an 'overdetermined system', as previously reviewed, since these are oftentimes computationally formidable problems with many possible solutions (too many to calculate 'exhaustively' – that is to say, in entirety).

Simply stated, like any model, OLSR begins with data and a hypothesis. A line drawn through the plotted data (as happened when working with quill and ink) represents this hypothesis, which typically attempts to predict otherwise unknown output based on the value(s) of known input. The iterative nature of OLSR becomes apparent as additional data accrue to the developing model, which must adjust to this new input. OLSR accommodates these adjustments by calculating the regression, determining the distance of each data point from this ideal line of performance, squaring, summing and then finally, taking the square root of resultant deviations or error.

This refinement step repeats iteratively to analyze all inbound data while continually adjusting its regression line to reduce the total squared error of the model, as compared to its target system. Upon successful completion of this operation, by definition, the line should ideally represent maximal signal and minimal noise.

Model Assumptions/Restrictions

Because statistical models are *never* the reality, each operates based on simplified assumptions. Each assumption is also a weakness or vulnerability of the method, as well.

OLSR is no exception. This form of regression requires: 1) uncorrelated observed errors; 2) a zero-mean among observed errors; 3) constant variance among observed errors ('*homoscedasticity*'); and 4) all observed error to be attributable to variation among latent variables, only.

When Assumptions/Restrictions Fail

When these assumptions and/or restrictions fail, the result is some form of generalization error. Recall, models that present more parameters than features may demonstrate excessive complexity and, thus, suffer from 'overfit' – this form of generalization error is primarily due to excessive variance in the model. Alternatively, models that present more features than parameters may suffer from excessive simplicity, resulting in an 'underfit' condition – generalization error primarily attributable to excessive bias.

When such systems require similar analysis, alternate methods may suffice. Accordingly, the next section advances to a discussion of 'Ridge Regression', an extension of OLSR and an example of L2-norm regularization.

Use Cases in Marketing and Sales

The ability to analyze large, chaotic, sociologically-derived datasets presents enormous potential, as applied to problems related to a variety of marketing and sales endeavors.   Given Google's vast influence within the domain, this is perhaps understandable, but their business is a business of people – more specifically, it is a business of *context* and *semantics*, because this is what differentiates human language (and experiences) from something machinelike and invariant.   For example, these are the concepts that determine if the term 'bill' relates to a 'bill of a goods' or 'a person/object named bill' – or a duck's bill, for that matter.

Given the continual compilation of vast and current retail databases, opportunity abounds.   These predictors are especially suited to managing the *lifetime value* of a consumer, which is a measure of the total cost/benefit derived from long-term consumer interactions. Many large corporations optimize profit by discarding non-cost-effective customers, which is inevitably a most delicate decision.

Related, the concept of *churn* quantifies a *stream of commerce* interaction with consumers that tallies completed/uncompleted transaction patterns.   A retail organization might benefit from carefully managing special officers to near-purchase contexts sufficient to induce a sale from conditions that previously generated a 'walk away'. This is another sensitive decision point – as with the previous use cases, supervised machine learning with linear regression can help!

Lesson Conclusion

As regards its application to large, complex, naturally-derived datasets, a primary shortcoming of simple linear regression pertains to its lack of error minimization. Likewise, by modern standards, OLSR suffers from a lack of '*regularization*'. This is an algorithmic (automated) means of simplifying and/or refining a statistical model to reduce generalization error

Models that lack this capacity are prone to developing excessive simplicity (underfitting) or excessive complexity (overfitting). Ridge Regression is an essential linear regression protocol that overcomes some of these conditions by providing an efficient means of regularization.

Ordinary Least Squares Linear Regression

L2 – RIDGE REGRESSION

Lesson Overview

In many pertinent ways, '*Ridge Regression*' (*RR*) ('*Tikhonov Regularization*' or '*weight decay*') extends '*Ordinary Least Squares Regression*' (*OLSR*) while performing the same essential task. For purposes of this discussion, think of RR as '*regularized OLS*'. This form of regularization (the L2-norm) reduces generalization error without altering a model's complexity. Owing to effects of its functionality, the iterative refinements of RR tend to shrink model coefficients toward zero without actually driving them to this limit.

The primary benefit derived from an RR application derives from its ability to provide viable models to problems that invalidate key OLS assumptions. Chiefly, RR produces models applicable to datasets that demonstrate multicollinearity and/or heteroscedasticity. RR regularization is a form of '*Structural Risk Minimization*'.

Relevant Nomenclature

As previously stated, RR works to resolve erroneous assumptions within statistical models using a least squares framework. RR regularization performs this service by applying a '*weight coefficient*' to each of the model's hidden parameters, which in turn supports an iterative refinement of the model, itself, to include recalculation of its features followed by additional rounds of refinement. As this process continues, some of the model's hidden variables will reduce *toward* (but not *to*) zero. Since none of these values ever *actually* drop to null, an RR solution is '*non-sparse*', in that it returns a non-zero value for *all* of its hidden parameters. Thus, RR does *not* perform '*variable selection*' (or '*model simplification*').

A primary reason to apply RR as a predictive regression pertains to the differences between '*well-posed*' and '*ill-posed*' problems, as well as the way in which OLSR manages these conditions. Recall the previous review of these concepts, and remember that they basically describe the level of compliance between system and model.

Specifically, RR works well to replace OLSR where '*multicollinearity*' and '*heteroscedasticity*' confound a simple solution. Like all models, RR presents limitations, as well, which the following sections will review.

To avoid introducing bias due to scaling within the input dataset, regularizers work best when applied to data that have been '*standardized*'. This process is similar to that of '*normalization*'. The effort here focuses on adjusting independent variables to scale while centering them with a variance of one.

For example, imagine a sample of numeric values that demonstrates a wide spread – some values are large and some small, although all relate to one another in some fashion. Extreme examples within the set may produce excessive (or, alternately, insufficient) influence in the final model, if analyzed as 'raw' (un-standardized, un-normalized) data. One solution, here, might include summing and dividing the data to represent each point as a 'share' or 'ratio' of overall input. Once the modeler centers and scales all data for the same variance (a variance of one), then each point of input will contribute to model development in a 'normalized' or 'standardized' way.

Overview (Ridge Regression)

At its core, '*Ridge Regression*' (*RR*) is, essentially, an '*Ordinary Least Squares Regression*' (*OLS* or *OLSR*) with an added feature – that of '*regularization*'. As such, this model largely relies on the same statistical assumptions – except for its tolerance of '*multicollinearity*' and/or '*heteroscedasticity*'. RR's popularity probably derives from ubiquitous presence of these confounding factors within the large, chaotic, naturally-derived datasets that offer so much promise to Deep Learning model developers.

Despite its tolerance of these effects, '*linearity*', '*independence*' and '*constant variance*' continue to be prime considerations for RR suitability as a predictive model. In particular, the latter requirement leaves RR somewhat sensitive to the inclusion of outliers – where these extreme values cannot be ignored or standardized away, then the model may demonstrate undue impact from their inclusion in the dataset (the forewarned student will perhaps anticipate the subject matter of a subsequent section of this course).

Selection of Ridge Regression

The informed statistician will select RR to perform a multiple regression on data that are multicollinear and/or heteroscedastic. OLSR will provide an unbiased model of these datasets, but the output of these ill-fitted solutions will likely demonstrate excessive bias. However, this being the case, selection of RR should not be a casual or trivial matter – rather, its selection should be need-based and fully cognizant of other viable alternatives.

For example, prior to relying upon RR to resolve all a model's ills, an informed designer may choose to simply collect more data to obtain a broader spread of observations (thus, somewhat negating the effect of multicollinearity). The designer may also elect to choose an alternate modeling method, one that provides a means of variable selection (via application of the L1-norm, perhaps). Finally, the compromising statistician can sometimes just remove the collinear observations, provided these data points are amenable to such treatment.

When they are not and these other options cannot suffice, then RR is a next-best choice. The reason for this discrimination derives from RR's functionality, which introduces additional artificial data ('*lambda*' or '*shrinkage coefficient*') into the problem to support a new form of sampling from its distributions. This synthetic insertion may be controversial within some professional settings, thus requiring careful deliberation prior to implementation.

Ridge Regression and OLS

The '*Variance Inflation Factor*' (*VIF*) provides a general 'rule of thumb' measurement for determining whether or not a model will benefit from RR. As previously stated, RR begins as an OLSR. Within a basic OLSR, the '*R*' parameter serves as a correlation matrix of the model's independent variables (hidden parameters), and its 'R^2' '*correlation variance*' coefficient doubles as the VIF. Within the multiple regression, an individual VIF of 10 (which corresponds to an R^2 of 0.90) tends to indicate the presence of excessive multicollinearity. Thus, the need for something like Ridge Regression.

Ridge Regression, Post-OLS Operations

Again, building upon the previous description of OLSR operations, RR initiates as such. During the regression, however, RR adds a small value, '*lambda*', to the correlation matrix '*diagonals*' ('*self-identities*' or '*self-correlations*') – indeed, this process gives RR its name, since the diagonal forms a kind of 'ridge' through the matrix. Hence, '*Ridge Regression*'. Typically, lambda is a positive quantity less than one (and usually less than 0.3). During iterative refinement of the model, this form of '*L2 regularization*' (RR) forces the sum of squared coefficients to be less than a preset value. By repeatedly setting, calculating and recalculating the model's distributions as associated with various values of lambda, RR seeks solution '*optima*' (highest of highs and/or lowest of lows). This search, then, provides a basic means for supervising the model's training experience (learning process), as it continually attempts to fit the data while reducing generalization error.

Overview (Lambda)

As applied to a Ridge Regression, the value choice for '*lambda*' (the '*ridge estimator*' or '*shrinkage parameter*') is a crucial trade-off, since an optimal value in this regard will produce a model with superior (reduced) error as compared to a model derived from OLS. Of course, a poor choice will likely produce a model that performs *worse* than an OLSR.

The *true* value of lambda depends upon its current targets of estimation, which are the hidden variables/parameters embedded within the underlying analytical system. These are the very parameters that the model trains to identify, and some if not all will likely represent truth within some measure of error. If the developer chooses a value for lambda that is greater than the truth, then the result will likely be a model demonstrating excessive bias (underfit from an OLS-perspective). Conversely, a small (or zero) value for lambda will likely produce a model that demonstrates excessive predictive variance (OLS overfit).

Unfortunately, no analytical solution *guarantees* discovery of an optimal lambda – this is one of RR's trade-offs. Based largely on its use of a squares-based method for error reduction, the RR method can only explore its analytical landscape during an iterative search for true coefficient values – the result is a 'best effort' and not a 'definitive' value for analytical coefficients. Again, because this search only *approaches* zero, the RR process will not remove unnecessary coefficients from the model, although their values may approach null, thereby greatly limiting their influence on model output.

Ridge Trace

Because it provides a useful service and, as such, often appears in machine learning discussions, the student will benefit from a summary review of the Ridge Trace method for calculating optimal lambda values. As a graphical method, Ridge Trace represents the Least Squares (LS) solution on its vertical axis, while its horizontal axis represents a relevant range for lambda. The iterative plot of variable values based on variation of lambda produces a series of curves that should tend to plateau (stabilize). The point in the chart at which all (or most) plots have achieved this property suggests an optimal value for lambda.

While this is an older method and, as such, not recommended for modern implementations, Ridge Trace remains useful as a tool for visualizing the complex relationship between lambda, RR and the truth of an analytical system. Although Ridge Trace can be used to supervise the training of a linear regression model, this is not state-of-the-art. Instead, most developers prefer to employ cross-validation to achieve the same effect.

Cross-Validation in Supervised Learning

'*Cross-validation*' describes the iterative process of validating a machine learning model. This is, essentially, a method for continually assessing a model's generalization error – that is, recall, the tradeoff space between the bias and variation apparent in a model's performance, as specifically applied to predictive regression problems.

In its essence, this procedure simply splits a machine learning dataset into two portions. The exact ratios of this split vary according to design criteria, but '*Zipf's Law*' provides a general rule of thumb at 80% training and 20% testing. The cross-validation process continues iteratively until the difference between training and testing output reduces to some required level (without inducing overfit). This process, then, represents a parametric search for optima within the system.

Understanding Ridge Regression

Currently, two theoretical schools of thought attempt to resolve core operability within the RR process. While a full review of Bayesian methods extends far beyond the scope of this work, the following passages offer a summarized explanation of this "school of thought" on the subject.

The Bayesian perspective frames RR according to standard constraints of the LS and OLS method – chiefly, this view indicates that RR resolves ill-posed problems by assuming that both data and model (coefficient/variable) values demonstrate a zero mean, variable independence and constant standard deviations, all or none of which might actually be true. RR further assumes heteroscedasticity and the presence of multicollinearity within the dataset. Given these constraints, RR produces the most probable solution to the given system, which its output expresses as the *a priori distribution* of the variables according to '*Bayes' Theorem*'. Crudely stated, Bayes' theorem describes a system for determining probabilities related to the occurrence of one phenomenon based on some known aspect of the phenomenal system – oftentimes the '*Bayesian prior probabilities*' are known (how many hits a baseball player has historically produced) while the '*Bayesian posterior probabilities*' are predicted (how likely the player is to make a hit at next bat, within a range of error, given this record).

In certain circumstances, the synthetic insertion and utilization of the 'lambda' value – with all its subsequent observations – may become problematic.   In these circumstances, critics may argue that this arbitrary manipulation acts to invalidate the resulting model. For this reason, use of RR (and similar solutions) should follow a diligent review of its benefits and detriments.

At the least, RR provides a means for reducing generalization error within a model's predictions. While this method enhances OLSR by providing a means for regularization by optimizing and reducing bias, RR provides no support for variable selection (reduction of model complexity).   Instead, RR is said to 'optimize' complexity, rather than 'reduce' it.

Use Cases in Sentiment Analysis

Ultimately, consumer-to-vendor interactions, whatever their nature, derive from an interplay of '*sentiment*'. Improved sentiment often equates to improved sales; conversely, any automated means of analyzing for this most subjective human quality should enhance a vendor's capacity to manipulate sentiment to benefit profits. Again, this is perhaps another reason for Google's monolithic presence in the field, since their roots lie in presenting the very best sentiment-based output to their consumers. In other words, Google learned what its customers wanted to know faster than any other competitor and they presented this content more accurately and precisely than any other.

Today, machine learning makes frequent appearance in the lives of countless consumers. '*Sentiment analysis*' plays a large role in '*recommendation services*', as demonstrated most popularly by the Internet Movie Database (IMDB), Amazon and a host of other powerhouse enterprises. Again, these are often understatedly delicate problems – embarrassments regularly make the news. Indeed, privacy concerns are enormous. More pertinently, when the underlying decision is well-made, profits rise due to improved consumer satisfaction derived from the tangible aspects of such an interaction, as well as its intangible benefits, too. After all, many consumers respond positively to a '*personalized shopping experience*' – though it some find it 'creepy' – once more, supervised machine learning with linear regression can help!

Lesson Conclusion

Recall the applications and qualifications that underly efficacious application of OLSR methods. Further recall how Ridge Regression (RR) extends OLSR functionality by providing a means for regularization to address the presence of multicollinearity and/or heteroscedasticity within the dataset of interest. In this way, RR resolves overfit attributable to OLSR models that fail according to invalidation of its underlying assumptions, by optimizing predictive bias without providing a means for variable selection. RR represents a means of L2-norm regularization.

Where the developer must reduce model complexity, another mode of regularization will be of benefit. This is the L1-norm mode, as exemplified by LASSO (more commonly of late, Lasso) Regression, reviewed next.

L2 – Ridge Regression

L1 – LASSO REGRESSION

Lesson Overview

Like Ridge Regression (*RR*), '*Least Absolute Shrinkage and Selection Operator*' ('*LASSO*' or, common nowadays, '*Lasso*') extends '*Ordinary Least Squares Regression*' (OLS or OLSR) by reducing the complexity of a model's input via application of a selective regularization method, as contained within the model algorithm. Unlike RR, Lasso provides a means for both optimizing *and* reducing model complexity due to its capacity as an L1-norm method (RR is L2-norm). Recall RR-optimized coefficients only *approach* zero values. Lasso's use of '*Manhattan Distance*' (or '*taxicab distance*'), rather than '*Euclidean Distance*' (as with RR), serves to drive overfit-inducing hidden variables to zero (or some fixed value), thus effectively removing them from the model. This, then, is a primary benefit of Lasso and the L1-norm.

Overview (Lasso)

Again, as with RR, Lasso essentially extends OLSR to address the presence of '*heteroscedasticity*' within a dataset that is otherwise amenable to these simpler analyses (although these models are not the optimal solution where '*multicollinearity*' exists). Lasso proceeds as RR, except the formulation of its regularization forces the sum of squared coefficients to be less than a set value (usually provided at runtime). During the iterative refinement process, this constraint induces the Lasso algorithm to set some model coefficients to zero (where RR only *approaches* zero), and it is this partial parametric drive to zero that provides Lasso's means of variable selection (complexity reduction).

Understanding Lasso Regression

As with RR, multiple schools of thought explore Lasso Regression's utility. Recall, model assumptions/constraints represent a key aspect of both L1- and L2-norm operations.

The geometric interpretation is probably the easiest to visualize. RR and Lasso require that both data and model (coefficient/variable) values demonstrate a zero mean, variable independence and constant standard deviations. When plotted about the origin, L1-norm error distributions produce a 'square' or 'diamond' shape having its corners on each of the four axes, while L2-norm error distributions plot as a circle on the same graph. Given its linear nature, the regression line will likely intersect with these features in subtly but vitally different ways. The former is likely to cross the error distribution at an axial corner (thus producing the variable-selecting zero value), while the latter will likely make off-axis, tangential contact with L2-norm's circular distribution, a process that drives resultant coefficient values toward zero without actually achieving true zero.

Like RR, Lasso Regression also benefits from a Bayesian interpretation. Where RR executes against a normal distribution of priors, Lasso represents a linear regression that demonstrates a Laplace distribution among variable priors. Somewhat dissimilar to the '*normal distribution*' ('*bell curve*'), a '*Laplace distribution*' is sharply peaked at zero while concentrating its probability mass closer to zero than the normal distribution. Thus, the Bayesian perspective also attempts to explain the L1-norm provision of variable selection, as described above.

As with all models – which are inherently limited in *some* fashion, since they are *never* the reality – Lasso Regression comes with constraints. Primarily, its functionality provides for scenarios that produce multiple, non-unique optimal solutions (*i.e.*, the solution is ill-posed).

Additionally, its application domain becomes limited when the input dataset is large, sparse (that is, presenting few examples among many possibilities) and high-dimensional. Combined together, these conditions describe the so-called '*large-p, small-n*' problem. Stated otherwise, this condition means the problem presents many features but few data points; consequently, the analytical system demonstrates too few observations to adequately cover the full scope of possible solutions.

Again, largely due to its provision for variable selection, Lasso regression saturates when applied to such problems, a feature that limits its output to a number of variables equivalent to sample size ('n'), which is, in these conditions, overwhelmed by the number of parameters in the model. Additionally, where multiple variables are well correlated, Lasso Regression only selects one (or a few) representatives of these contributors, when so constrained – a feature that obviously reduces model fidelity, especially where the individual parameters are of interest.

Lasso Variants

Due to Lasso's utility as a means of reducing model complexity, multiple variants of the method attempt to overcome one or more of its limitations (perhaps by inserting into the solution additional or alternate limitations). In this regard, Lass is no exception, and the student will benefit from a brief review of these concepts, as follows. (*NOTE: while mathematics and formulae are not the focus of this executive review, this subject matter may warrant a more applied external review, given its potential benefits to the student.*)

From a certain perspective, '*Group Lasso*' is essentially a Lasso Regression with an additional Ridge-Regression-like regularization step. Group Lasso proceeds as a standard Lasso Regression, except it uses a pair of matrices (tables) in place of a pair of single-dimensional coefficients, as per standard Lasso. In effect, these matrices represent pre-defined 'groups' of variables, such that performance of the Group Lasso method first identifies and correlates these variables accordingly – at this level of selection and refinement, the algorithm uses an L2-norm (as demonstrated by RR) that prevents complete elimination of these sub-level parameters. Thus, with the proper choice of Group Lasso settings, the standard Lasso selection transpires across the groups-of-variables (matrices) rather than individual variables, thereby selecting *all* members of a group, or not. Hence the label, 'Group Lasso'. A number of Group Lasso subvariants are also available, each expanding on the process in subtle ways that lie beyond the scope of this work.

'*Sparse Group Lasso*' extends Group Lasso by adding an additional RR-like penalty coefficient to the matrix-level sub-group selection process. This protocol supports *selection* of individual covariates *within* groups. Further extending this concept, '*Group Lasso with Overlap*' provides a means of *sharing* covariates *between* groups.

The '*Fused Lasso*' method also presents interesting possibilities that make it worthy of a passage here. Though its fundamental operations differ from the 'Group Lasso' protocol, Fused Lasso performs a similar service, in that it provides a means of predefining temporal or spatial constraints within the analytical system, which loosely collects associated data into temporally or spatially oriented groups or 'clusters' (in fact, a Fused Lasso variant, Cluster Lasso, enhances this 'clustering' effect of the algorithm to support categorical manipulations). This vital service, in turn, then supports a process of regularization (normalization or smoothing) of the input, based on its relationship to the temporal/spatial dimension of the solution space. Thus, Fused Lasso reduces uninteresting variation attributable to wide fluctuations of time or space.

Use Cases in Security

As with many unpleasant human endeavors, to include the gamut of security matters from frontline combat to frontline fraud detection, oftentimes long hours of idle, uneventful boredom meet moments of brazen violence, theft or some other malicious activity. Beyond human concerns, nature presents a constant challenge to the safety and wellbeing of human beings and their infrastructure.

Through the nineties and the early part of this century, a number of security-related technologies blossomed. High-definition cameras observe virtually every aspect of many large, vulnerable installations, to include entire sectors of cities like New York and London. Increasingly capable Deep Learning (DL) software now couples with these devices to provide real-time surveillance via *augmented reality*. Port authorities and transportation safety agencies around the globe now employ powerful CT (*Computed Tomography*) scanners to examine baggage with unprecedented multidimensional detail. *'Millimeter wave'* technology permits similar access to the external person of passing commuters, but with huge caveats of privacy and government overreach.

The effort here is to provide a high-throughput, non-intrusive means that requires little to no *'divestiture'* (removal of clothing or personal possessions) while affording minimal assault to human dignity. Machine learning shines here, since the incredible volume of security-related information – the very volume and complexity that previously rendered these data sources intractable to all but living human intervention – is now amenable to the analysis of DL software. To be certain, these are often complex models that transcend the subject matter of this course, but these concepts appear repeatedly throughout the struggle to *make accurate, precise decisions* about the results of such systems.

Security datasets are sparse datasets, by nature. Many hours of boredom punctuated by minutes of stark terror, as it were, explicitly requires that the system monitor, be it man or machine, must review volumes of input prior to making a single practical, actionable decision. Then again, this decision is not simply the detection of an action – that is, the '*reactive*' security measure, which includes first-responders and the like – this is also the detection of '*anomalies*' – the thing 'out of place', the unusual circumstance, which is only defined by all those hours of normalcy and boredom. By definition, an effective '*anomaly detector*' is a '*proactive*' means of security.

By monitoring standard flows of traffic and communications, a DL system can learn the typical patterns prevalent within a given environment to report rare disturbances to a much more effectively utilized human in the loop oversight. This is a person who is not tethered and tasked with watching an endless bank of monotonously routine video feeds, rather, this is a single on-call technician responding to highly targeted, accurate and precise alerts, thus disposing of the long hours of boredom part (and the associated manhours, wasted part, too). Whether within the DL models while training or when serving as standalone models, too, supervised learning and linear regression is playing active roles in these advancements.

Lesson Conclusion

Thus far, this course has presented a story of progression. From simple linear regression, through ordinary least squares, Ridge Regression and now Lasso Regression and its variants, the student might recognize a centralized trend to the discussion. Specifically, the primary focus of the developing plot lands squarely upon the application of these concepts as supervised learning models.

Of course, a deeper sub-plot runs through the discourse, as well, since the specter of all things 'Machine Learning' and 'Deep Learning' (DL) lingers nearby. Where RR and Lasso Regression speciate into ever more subtle, powerful and discriminatory variants, this developmental trajectory closely tracks with the always expanding frontier of deep neural network applications. There, developers struggle to apply high-dimensional models to high-dimensional problem spaces that are also oftentimes quite sparse. This is a search of searches among graphs of graphs and the theoretical space is so vast that efficiencies and optimizations present premium rewards for discovery, since analytical truth is rare and well-hidden.

Perhaps an ideal solution should function at the level of the overall DL architecture as well as it functions at the level of the finest branching node. Thus, the algorithm should adaptively make selections within selections while identifying groups within groups, optimizing its optimizations and/or smoothing its own smoothness. This may sound a bit poetic, but the perception is accurate.

Recall how Lasso (and RR) extends 'Ordinary Least Squares Regression' (OLSR) and recall Lasso's demonstration of the L1-norm as compared to RR's demonstration of the L2-norm. Recall the way in which

Lasso variants extend these operations by providing and/or linking covariate groups to the analysis.

All of these measures attempt to improve data fit at the finest possible level without inducing overfit and while reducing Generalization Error – that is, error attributable to bias and/or variance. Finally, recognize the benefits and differences identifiable with the L1-norm (complexity optimization *and* complexity reduction) and the L2-norm (complexity optimization, only).

These are all common themes in the expansion of discussion that follows, and these concepts also represent points of order that frequently arise during the DL/ML design process. Ultimately, however, as with all models, Lasso Regression suffers from limitations. Specifically, its variable-selection feature becomes problematic when applied under sparse, highly- and multiply-correlated variable conditions. As with Group Lasso, a combination of L1- and L2-norm operations might prove beneficial. This is the realm of 'Elastic Net Regression'.

L1 + L2 – ELASTIC NET REGRESSION

Lesson Overview

'*Elastic Net Regression*' (*ENR*) extends both Ridge Regression (RR) and Lasso Regression (LR) in that this method provides an iterative and serial combination of L1- and L2-norm functionality. In this way, ENR adds a '*quadratic*' component, called '*alpha*', to the existing Lasso-style (L1-norm) regularization penalty, '*lambda*', thus rendering the overall loss function '*convex*' (*i.e.*, the function ensures a unique optimum, which transforms a potentially ill-posed problem into a well-posed variant). If this sounds impressive, perhaps too much so, relax – the quadratic part (meaning 'squares-related' part) simply refers to application of an L2-norm regularization step, which, by itself, is simply a Ridge Regression.

Relevant Nomenclature

As a term, the word '*quadratic*' merely refers to anything that is '*squares-based*'. By now, the vigilant student should think 'L2-norm' upon mention of the word 'square'.

Related, the concepts of '*convexity*' and '*concavity*', as pertains to a discussion of loss functions (in this case, specifically those derived from linear regression models), marks the difference between a solution with a unique optimum solution, or not, respectively. Think of these different shapes and then identify the 'highpoints' of each. The former presents a single highest point (its center), while the latter presents an infinite number (its rim). Thus, a '*convex*' solution space differs markedly from its '*concave*' example.

Finally, the following discussion makes references to concepts labeled '*singularities*' and/or '*vertices*'. Specifically, this phenomenon derives from a visual depiction of the L1- *versus* L2-norm error distribution (or *penalty space*) as it applies to regularization. Recall that the L1-norm in this context describes a square (or diamond) centered about the origin (0,0 in cartesian coordinates) with its points on the vertical and horizontal axes. Where the corners of this square distribution meet the axes, then, these locations identify solutions that are '*singularities on the vertices*' –the regression line will likely intersect with this space at the axes, thus producing a unique optimal solution to the problem while also tending to drive at least some variables to zero-values. In contrast, the L2-norm error distribution centers about the origins in a circular fashion, such that it presents a uniform aspect regardless of rotation about the origins, a feature that presents, potentially, infinite possible optima.

Overview (Elastic Net Regression [ENR])

As previously stated, Elastic Net Regression (ENR) extends RR and Lasso, which, in turn, extend the OLSR method. ENR is an iterative, two-way model-refinement process, in that ENR proceeds as a standard Ridge Regression at the initiation of each iterative round of RR-type (L2-norm) optimization, which concludes with a Lasso-type (L1-norm) shrinkage operation. Thus, ENR, as an algorithm, ingests two '*lambda*' coefficients (imaginatively labeled '*lambda-1*' and '*lambda-2*'), which represent the RR and the Lasso penalties, respectively, along with an '*alpha coefficient*' that describes the applied distribution of L2-versus L1-norm regularization. Here, an alpha value of 0 indicates a pure RR analysis, while an alpha of 1 represents pure Lasso; otherwise, alpha provides for a weighted blend of the two (*e.g.*, an alpha of 0.5 would indicate an equal blend of both).

In this way, ENR benefits from the computationally efficient L2-norm optimization, while also providing a means of variable selection via application of a subsequent L1-norm regularization. As previously described, the model developer will balance this meter (as well as her selection of lambda-1 and lambda-2) via iterative rounds of cross-validation, post-training.

Understanding ENR

Obviously, ENR represents a hybrid solution that attempts to balance application of L1- and L2-norm regularizations. The easiest way to understand ENR operations continues the graphical description already provided for L1 and L2 (which theoreticians often depict as a diamond and circle pattern of error distribution centered about the origins of a

2D graph). As a hybrid, the ENR error space might resemble a lozenge shape – a square with rounded sides or a circle with corners focused at the axes ('singularities at the vertices'). Thus, ENR simultaneously provides both optimization and simplification services. Finally, like Group Lasso, which specifically forces correlation groupings via use of matrix variables, ENR naturally provides a grouping/clustering service, as well.

Again, as with all models, ENR presents limitations. While it performs well in sparse, heteroscedastic and/or multicollinear problem spaces, as with Group Lasso, ENR still suffers from biased selection of highly correlated variables. *I.e.*, the Lasso portion of the regularization process tends to select one member from each of its naturally-defined (as opposed to user-defined) groups while ignoring the rest.

Course Concepts, Revisited

Repetition is memory's friend. According to this philosophy, then, the student will benefit from briefly revisiting the core principles described, thus far.

First, discussion began by describing Ordinary Least Squares Regression (OLSR), a simple machine learning method that provides a foundation for the lessons that followed. These models work well with datasets that demonstrate, among other previously described features, a lack of collinearity and heteroscedasticity.

Ridge Regression (RR) adds a squares-based (L2-norm based) regularization method to standard OLSR. Consequently, RR works well with datasets that present dense features, heteroscedastic and/or multicollinear variables.

Lasso Regression (LR) adds a Manhattan-distance-based (L1-norm based) regularization method to standard OLSR. As such, Lasso applies well to large datasets demonstrating sparse features, heteroscedastic data and that *lack* multicollinearity.

Finally, Elastic Net Regression (ENR) provides a combination of L2 and L1 regularization. This method applies well to datasets presenting sparse features, heteroscedastic data that are also multicollinear.

Use Cases in Temporal Analyses

A 'temporal' analysis is simply a study of time-related series of events. This should bring immediate thoughts to mind, since life is nothing more than a collection of temporal phenomena. Perhaps this is, in fact, a defining characteristic of the 'human condition', since we possess an apparently unique biological ability to retain and conceptualize the past, apply it to an understanding of our current state of being and then, using these two points of reference, foresee the future – at least, to some practical, non-mystical extent.

This is not, after all, clairvoyance. Not in the traditional sense of that word, at the least. Then again, as state-of-the-art advances – perhaps with the looming introduction of affordable quantum computing – this type of analysis presents a brass ring of sorts, because *everything* is temporal.

Prediction can be a static thing, of course, since, in many cases, the same 'y' always derives from a given 'x', as it were. These statistical instances are helpful, to be sure, since we need to know our velocity at any given moment when we are driving, same as we might need to occasionally mark the time of day. Yet, these bits of information become truly useful when we can put them together in some meaningful way to *anticipate* a profitable, or detrimental, situation.

Again, the subject matter is supervised learning with linear regression. The datasets are sparse, chaotic, presenting unknown features and demonstrating unknown relationships among these features. A model developer tasked with analyzing these systems needs a flexible, automated method for analyzing these signals, and the models described within this text will undoubtedly be popular choices, whether of loss functions, initializers, regularizers, activation functions and as models, in their own right.

L1 + L2 – Elastic Net Regression

Lesson Conclusion

Given the above re-visitation of course concepts, a pair of data-source-based application gaps might seem apparent. In fact, the L1+L2 combination of ENR specifically applies to datasets having sparse features, heteroscedastic and *some* collinear data. Datasets that are very large with sparse data, dense features and unknown internal structures and/or relationships will likely benefit from analyses developed for text-classification and Natural Language Processing (NLP) problems (not covered in this course).

Finally, datasets that are sparse in both data *and* features while presenting unknown structure and/or internal relations will benefit from a somewhat different class of solutions. Specifically, kernel-based and non-parametric regression methods perform well in this environment.

BEYOND L1 + L2 – NON-PARAMETRIC, KERNEL-BASED REGRESSION

Lesson Overview

Clearly, Ordinary Least Squares Regression (OLSR), Ridge Regression (RR), Lasso Regression (LR) and Elastic Net Regression (ENR) all benefit from a common etiology. While these commonalities are numerous, for the sake of the following discussion, a primary commonality relates to the way in which these algorithms constrain hypothesis space to assumptively simplify requisite analyses. This is, essentially, the 'common touch' with which these procedures sample the underlying analytical system. For example, OLSR and Lasso employ linear approaches, while RR and ENR use quadratic solutions.

As expected, the natural world is not so limited. Indeed, nature demonstrates countless meaningful relationships among its parts and pieces. Oftentimes, these relationships are poorly modeled by linear and/or quadratic means, if at all. Where these sensory methodologies fail – or perhaps where the model developer simply requires improved operational flexibility – another variety of model may suffice.

Non-parametric, kernel-based regressions provide this flexibility, both as a means of alternately 'sensing' the world and as a means of flexibility deploying a chosen modeling paradigm. These advanced methods improve data-based insight (as opposed to developer-based insight) into model structure as an added benefit to their deployment as machine learning models. Chiefly, this section describes '*Gaussian Process Regression*' (*GPR*) and various ensemble methods for deployment of these algorithms.

Relevant Nomenclature

Within the text that follows, a '*hyperplane*' is essentially a 'a subspace that is one dimension less than its ambient space'. For example, within 3D space, hyperplanes are 2D constructs; within 2D space, then, they are 1D constructs. Extrapolating to arbitrary dimensions, then, a given n-dimensional space will demonstrate hyperplanes of (n-1)-dimensions. For the sake of the following discussion, these concepts simply provide a means for describing hyper-dimensional distributions.

A word on this subject will benefit the student. Most human beings imagine one dimension without difficulty as a line, two dimensions as a plane and three dimensions as a cube. How does nature represent the fourth dimension? The fifth? Can the imaginative student imagine a representation of the eleventh dimension? Probably not – at least, not as the eleventh dimension actually seems (some physicists promote the idea of an eleven-dimensional reality comprised of ten space dimensions and a single time dimension). The astute student will promote video (a 3D holographic video, or reality, would be more accurate) as a representation of the fourth dimension, since these media depict a 3D-world moving through the fourth dimension of time – of course, video somewhat ironically accomplishes this as a 2D rendition!

These concepts quickly confuse. Fortunately, a simple trick helps frame the problem in more human terms. Rather than envisioning the fourth dimension as a temporal entity, instead think of it is as a 'line of boxes' or a 'stack of boxes'. Each 3D space is represented by the variations attributable to its vertical placement in the stack, which represents the fourth dimension. Now the fifth dimension can be visualized as a matrix of boxes – that is rows and columns of boxes, such that each 3D space is now represented by both its horizontal *and* vertical placement within the 'flat'. The sixth dimension is a box of boxes, and so on. While this vision of hyper-dimensionality does not really do justice to the way these data naturally 'fall-out' in any given natural system, as a conceptual anchor the student may at least use this perspective to understand how hyperplanes work to resolve the chaos of modern datasets.

Imagine, for example, a box of boxes – that is to say, a dataset that describes each data point by six dimensions. These need not be spatial or temporal dimensions, incidentally. In fact, most often they are not (since we only know three dimensions of space and one of time). Rather, a 'dimension' here is merely a quantifiable label ascribed to the data – *e.g.*, height, weight, hair-color, eye-color, nationality, gender, etc.... As described here, then (without the *et cetera* and all it implies) a dataset so designed would describe each of its entries according to these six dimensions, beginning with height and ending with gender. To see the entire dataset as a whole, the way nature intends, simply collapse all these transparent boxes-within-boxes and their datapoints into a single two-dimensional representation. What pattern does the data make? Probably one that resembles chaos, depending upon the dimensions chosen for this collapse (height by weight, weight by age, *etc...*). By expanding the data according to its dimensions, however, the curious student may begin to identify commonalities associated with the data points attributed to a specific label. For example, by selecting and reordering the 3D cubes according to the 'height' dimension, a quick glance at the resultant patterns might make clear within the system some influence of height that is not readily apparent from another perspective.

Once more, because machine learning tends to operate in this high-dimension space, the *'feature space'* of the model should, as closely as possible according to some *'mapping'* represent the *'original input space'* of the problem. In this context, 'feature space' is simply the collections of features used to characterize a given dataset – for example a dataset related to human beings might contain the features 'gender', 'height', 'weight' and 'age' – the values provided for these fields as per each individual recorded in the database, then, describe the 'feature space' of the problem. A model designer might need to describe the data in another way, perhaps expressing height and weight as a ratio labeled 'height-over-weight', which provides a feature with the same name that contains values 'mapped' from the original feature space into the new features space, such that 'height-over-weight' in the derived space simply represents the division of the original feature, 'height', by the original feature, 'weight'. This, then, is also its *'mapping'*.

From this perspective, the student should see hyperdimensional data spaces everywhere. Any modern sociological database will almost certainly be *'hyperdimensional'*.

Incidentally, a *'feature vector'* is simply a collection of features, as described above. *E.g.*, the parenthetical collection ('gender', 'height', 'weight', 'age') represents a feature vector. When manipulating vectors (and matrices), the multiplication of one same-size vector against another same-size vector produces a single quantity. This is a form of feature reduction. This is also an example of the *'dot-product'* operation.

Finally, in the context of the following discussion, a *'kernel'* is simply a function describing similarity over pairs of data points in their original representation. For the sake of the simplified discourse that follows, the key term here is 'function' – any viable function, at all (linear, quadratic, *etc*...). Within the machine learning domain, the '*Support Vector Machine*' (*SVM*) is a '*kernel method*' most often applied to categorical problems, though this tool also serves predictive needs, as well, with the proper choice of kernel.

These kernel functions operate in a high-dimensional, implicit feature space, but they do not compute data coordinates in these terms (which, in the case of an unknown system, would prove to be impossible, anyway). Instead, these kernel functions improve computational efficiency by simply calculating the inner dot-products between all pairs of data in the feature space (*i.e.*, in the, ideally, *reduced* feature space). This process is called the '*kernel trick*' and it lies at the heart of the concepts described within this section of the course.

Overview (Kernel Regression)

Simply stated, a '*kernel regression*' is a non-parametric method for estimating the conditional expectation of a random variable, given the value of a known (and, hopefully, related) variable. In other words, the expectation of 'Y' given 'X' is conditional on some function 'm' – this function 'm' represents an interchangeable component (a kernel) within the system. As such, these methods can identify non-linear relationships hidden within a dataset, given selection of an appropriate kernel.

Of primary benefit within the context of this course, these methods provide a kind of '*plug-n-play*' operability to standard regressions, which more readily facilitates rapid training and/or cross-validation of complex graphical models (*e.g.*, Deep Learning models) applied to datasets suspected to contain a variety of functional relationships (linear, quadratic, Gaussian, logistic, etc...).

Support Vector Machines (SVM)

While any kind of applicable software could conceivably implement a kernel regression, this course focuses on the deployment of a '*Support Vector Machine*' (*SVM*) to accomplish this task. Though SVMs more commonly appear as solutions to classification problems, these tools can also perform as predictors with the proper analytical approach and an appropriate choice of kernels. They operate by 'constructing' a hyperplane in high- or infinite-dimensional space, such that this hyperplane separates the data (in a classification problem) by the widest possible margin (the '*functional margin*'), since larger margins tend to lower generalization error.

SVMs as Kernel Machines

Although a given SVM implementation might easily use a linearly oriented kernel to perform its intended analysis, the full power of SVMs as '*Kernel Machines*' (*KM*) relates to their capacity to use virtually *any* similar function as a kernel. Again, the kernel acts to provide hyper-dimensional space to support definition of a practical hyperplane among the data.

Support Vector Regression (SVR)

Imagine stretching data like an elastic fishing net until the points of two contained categories fall to either side of a line as separated by an optimum (maximal) margin. From the perspective of the net, the result might represent a chaotic jumble, while the dividing line remains linear. In reality, when the net returns to its original shape (say, as seen splayed across the sand in a rough square), the same divider will no longer present a linear appearance – instead, from this point of view, the data appear ordered and the separator appears chaotic. Crudely represented, then, this is the trade between '*feature space*' and '*original input space*'; this is also a crude depiction of the hyperplane, itself, since it is, in fact, only a 'plane' (from the traditional definition) when observed from feature space. The translation – or mapping – from one space to the other is fully dependent upon the nature of the selected kernel. Thus, different kernels may develop widely varied solutions.

Popular Kernel Waveforms (Distributions)

Since each kernel is simply a function, and since functions support plotting of observations-versus-hidden parameters of the system, the observant student will probably most readily understand kernel functions by reviewing the shape (or '*waveform*') of each function's 2D graphical output. This section describes some of the more popular variations using a verbal method, but a quick online review will provide relevant images of these curves to aid comprehension.

The '*uniform kernel*' presents a rectilinear (rectangular) form, while the '*triangular kernel*' presents, oddly enough, a triangular form (sharply peaked upward at the origin). An '*Epanechnikov kernel*' produces a parabolic form. A '*quartic kernel*' demonstrates a bi-weight curve – this form resembles a steep hill with a dip in the top middle oriented around the vertical axis, while the '*tri-weight kernel*' displays as a steep hill with a steep, smooth rounded top, again oriented around the origin. A '*tricube kernel*' plots a similar steep hill, but one having a rather flatter top transition, while a '*Gaussian kernel*' simply represents the '*normal curve*' (or '*bell curve*' or '*normal distribution*'). '*Cosine kernels*' demonstrate a cosinus wave; '*logistic kernels*' and '*sigmoid function kernels*' exhibit 'S-shaped' curves that have upper and lower horizontal asymptotes, and, finally, graphical output from a '*Silverman kernel*' resembles the Gaussian output, albeit with a flatter overall aspect and straighter slopes.

Popular Kernels

As with individual kernel waveforms, a variety of kernel algorithms are available for design-time selection. The student will also benefit from a brief review of these algorithms. The Code Base and Appendix A contains a *very* simple graphical representation of these distributions.

The '*Fisher kernel*' supports generative classification and retrieval analyses. Essentially, this protocol quantifies the similarity between two objects based on sets of measurements derived from each object and a statistical model. This procedure determines the class for a new, as yet unclassified object by calculating an average of the '*Fisher kernel distance*' from the new object to every known member of a given class. The new object then identifies with the class that produces a minimized overall distance.

'*Graph kernels*' generally apply in structure mining scenarios as relates to quantifying the structure of graph models. This kernel performs a service similar to that of the Fisher kernel, except the resultant distance represents a node-by-node comparison of one graph to another. Final output is a value that quantifies the similarity of the graphs in question.

'*Kernel smoothers*' support machine learning model refinement. This technique estimates a function as the weighted average of neighboring observed data, where the kernel defines the specific weight value, such that closer points tend to receive higher weight values. The waveform is smooth, with the level of smoothness being set by a single parameter.

'*Polynomial kernels*' act as non-linear classifiers. These kernels represent vector (training sample) similarity in a feature space over polynomials derived from original variables, thus supporting machine learning of non-linear models. The polynomial kernel examines both individual and combinations of input samples. Within a regression, these are '*interaction features*', as described.

'*Radial basis function kernels*' serve to   classify objects and/or quantify their similarities based on their 'distance' from the origin (or some other defined point). These are, of course, Euclidean distances that tend to plot as circles, or clusters, oriented around the mean (L2-norm) or the median (L1-norm) of each distribution.

Finally, '*string kernels*' perform string-based clustering and classification analyses. This is a basic method for quantifying similarities between two strings of arbitrary and, probably, unequal length.

Overview (Gaussian Process)

A '*Gaussian process*' is simply a '*stochastic*' (random) process (*i.e.*, a collection of random variables indexed by time or space). As with natural data sources, finite collections of these variables tend to demonstrate normal ('bell curve') distributions. Crudely stated, this feature constrains hypothesis space via application of a 'normal' waveform, rather than a linear waveform (or functional distribution). Because most natural and sociological data derive from 'Gaussian processes', this kernel perhaps represent the generic example and, as such, benefits from widespread implementation within machine learning settings.

Gaussian Process Regression (Kriging)

'*Kriging*' or '*Gaussian process regression*' is a smoothing process typically applied to non-linear models using Gaussian '*interpolation*' (the process of constructing new data points within the range of a discrete set of known data points). This is simply the derivation of a linear model that 'flows' more smoothly between the boundaries derived by producing error-encompassing plots of linear function waveforms (that is, using both upper and lower bounds of error associated with the given trendline). Other interpolating methods are also commonly used, primarily to include '*spline*' based methods (a spline is a function or curve defined, or interpolated, piecewise by polynomials).

Understanding Gaussian Regression

The term '*Gaussian*', which derives from a man's name (*Carl Friedrich Gauss*, 1777-1855), may seem to be a terribly daunting term. In reality, even the casually interested student probably understands this principle well, because it represents one of the first lessons in science and/or statistical mathematics. Recall how random samples drawn from large, chaotic, naturally-derived datasets tend to produce a 'normal distribution' – that is a 'bell curve' distribution – which can describe many useful features of the underlying system. This 'bell curve' or 'normal distribution' is also a '*Gaussian distribution*', a '*Gaussian curve*' or a '*Gaussian function*'. So, a 'Gaussian kernel' simply 'senses' the system with this waveform as its primary constraint to the hypothetical solution space. Besides its general basis in the analysis of natural phenomena, within the context of model performance and, at a "higher level", Deep Learning network management, Gaussian systems support a wide array of proven methods for calculating mean, error margins, value estimates and more, features that improve model efficiencies, especially as relates to the training and testing process. Since Gaussian processes can represent an infinite-dimensional generalization of multivariate normal distributions, this kernel's popularity derives from its subsequent ability to improve model fit as applied within unknown systems.

Ensemble Methods

Model '*ensembles*' are popular solutions to complex problems. Perhaps this is as should be, since human cognition is unquestionably an ensemble, of sorts – probably an ensemble of ensembles of ensembles... Within the context of this subject matter, supervised learning with linear regression, ensembles come in two flavors, '*averaged*' and '*boosted*'.

Ensembles that employ an '*averaging method*' typically construct, train and test multiple, independent models, oftentimes comprised of unique architectures. The 'averaging' aspect of these protocols usually pertains to the average of the ensemble's predictions, which serves to reduce variance as compared to single-point predictors. Averaging may also take place at various layers/levels of the model and the averaging, itself, may be conducted in a variety of design-dependent fashions, to include the use of 'bagging methods', 'forests of random trees' and many others – all of which are, essentially (for the sake of this discussion) procedures for grouping the entities to be included in the averaging operation.

Ensembles that employ a '*boosting method*' typically construct a series of models in sequential fashion, each trained independently to produce a collective 'consensus' prediction/classification. The primary goal of this approach is to reduce bias in the combined output. Boosted ensembles typically attempt to combine several 'weak' models into something with significant capacity.

Use Cases in Asset Management and Logistics

Amazon and Walmart, among others, make the case for tight efficiencies associated with management of assets, inventories and the logistic systems that transform raw materials into profit. Increasingly popular, the so-called 'Internet of Things' (IoT) provides an increasingly connected world, one envisioned long ago by science-fiction masters such as Phillip K. Dick and his thriller entitled "Minority Report", which actually describes a kind of machine intelligence that provides a Bayesian-like output to security forces tasked with stopping crime *before* it happens.

Asset management is more than counting boxes on shelves. 'Asset maintenance' performed via IoT analyses will enable real-time, *proactive* insight and intervention into logistic and asset management systems – in contrast, the *reactive* ('forensic') response is most common today. These enterprises all provide temporally delimited sparse datasets with all the other characteristics that make them so attractive to modern machine learning developers.

Likewise, logistics is more than scheduling pickups and deliveries. Accuracies count, yet these systems must be capable of analyzing the holistic logistics enterprise, from the 'stream of commerce' at retail counters, through the warehouse to the individual driver and truck – millions of transactions and interactions per day (or per hour). The volume and chaos of these datasets previously befuddled application of 'traditional', 'rule-based', 'hard-coded' algorithms, but have since become the untapped potential of a generation.

Finally, much like the security use-cases previously described, many aspects of asset management and logistics are matters of long-hours-of-boredom, and on. It is the 'brief moments' of concern that, again, make something like '*outage prediction*' formerly a matter of pure human-in-the-loop intervention. After all, most manufactured 'things' are produced to last, but only for so long. Given the chaos of nature, countless influences determine the longevity of production equipment and the personnel tasked with keeping it all going. Through the near future, supervised learning with linear regression will influence these decisions, both of the automated and human-derived variety.

Lesson Conclusion

As previously stated, the preceding discussion attempts to describe progress through both the data space and the applicable model space. The primary undertaking is the development of evermore capable and powerful models to address applications of increasingly voluminous, sparse and chaotic data sources that also demonstrate increasingly unknown features and relationships. Within any given multi-dimensional dataset, various relationships exhibiting various properties may arise. Traditionally, developers entered the model design process with considerable information about the data (that is, 'metadata') already in pocket. Modern datasets are simply too complex for this kind of manual approach to make practically efficient progress.

At the same time, the deployment of an inflexible machine learning architecture is probably not an optimal solution, either. As the preceding discussion has explored, modern designers benefit from a wide selection of statistical tools, each tailored to a specific interest – or, as the case may be, sufficiently generalized to support meaningful, if sub-optimal, preliminary exploration of almost any dataset (as with the Gaussian kernel, for example). Results of these initial, crude analytical passes may sufficiently inform the use of various models and/or kernels intended to better approximate the system and refine model-to-data fit.

Given the explicit nature of the applicable problem domain, applications of supervised machine learning abound. To improve professional and theoretical orientation, the interested student will benefit from a brief review of key solutions in the domains of healthcare, education, financial services, retail and the travel/entertainment enterprise.

APPLICATIONS IN THE HEALTHCARE, EDUCATION, FINANCIAL SERVICES, RETAIL AND TRAVEL ENTERPRISE

Beyond L1 + L2 – Non-Parametric Regression

Lesson Overview

This course began with a brief review of the benefits, and limitations, of 'traditional', 'rule-based', 'hard-coded' statistical models developed manually for application against relatively simple problem spaces (as compared to modern 'big data' sources). Unfortunately, given historical limitations of practical theory and computational capacity, many interesting datasets remained opaque to such analyses.

With the 2015 release of TensorFlow and the subsequent flood of competing machine learning, artificial intelligence and/or deep learning tools, these solutions became viable analytical choices for the first time. Additionally, these advanced models shine when applied to the intractable problems previously described. Quite recently, then, very large datasets of unknown data- and/or feature-densities having additionally unknown structure and/or relationships established between these features.

The preceding sections of this course review a variety of regression-based supervised machine learning protocols applicable to such datasets. Indeed, anywhere natural, sociological data meets predictive needs and profit potential, the described methods will find a lucrative role. This section touches upon some of these implementations to improve student orientation with the professional domain and, thereby, enhance his or her ability to anticipate useful trends within the overlying technical enterprise.

SML in Healthcare

The healthcare industry presents *enormous* opportunities for application of machine learning models, since the primary focus of this business is human beings, their needs, physical conditions, financial wellbeing, health, *et cetera*. Given the fact that almost everyone will present in healthcare setting at some point in their existence, these data sources tend to be large, dynamic and packed with potential for profit and humanitarian benefit. Consequently, multiple efforts apply supervised machine learning methods with linear regression to achieve a variety of analytical goals.

For example, a 2017 project used these methods to predict healthcare costs based on past performance of services as described within a large database. This solution determined that Artificial Neural Networks (ANNs) regularized with gradient boosting produce the most accurate and precise predictions of performance for low to medium cost patients. High cost patient performance benefits most from application of an ANN regularized with Ridge Regression.

A more recent 2018 project used a regularized supervised learning method to predict production failures related to pharmaceutical manufacturing processes. In fact, a 2018 state of the art review determined that 42% of these supervised machine learning implementations within the healthcare industry utilized SVMs as Kernel Machines to perform these analyses, while 31% used Neural Networks (NNs, the remainder being minimally divided among a wide array of options).

SML in Education

Another industry primarily devoted to the care and feeding of human beings – and, as such, subject to the collection of large, sociologically-derived datasets – educational concerns also benefit from the rise of supervised machine learning applications. Multiple 2018 initiatives describe progress in this regard.

Combinations of the linear regression models previously described herein provide a means of predicting human behavior via analysis of large, sparse, heteroscedastic and/or multicollinear datasets to anticipate individual scholastic trajectories, this providing an efficacious means for determining the presentation of granular, personal-interest-focused educational content thereto.

Indeed, these models also support the actual generation of this content, as well, based on predictions of market need, student interests and the like, all as applied to the mining of vast multimedia corpora of knowledge (*e.g.,* Wikipedia.com). Extending these services beyond the basic academic track, educational institutions also use this technology to provide operational feedback and personalized content straight through graduation to include career guidance and career-track-based content generation, as well.

SML in Financial Services

Again, the common theme of sociologically-derived datasets appears within the context of problems related to the financial services industry. In 2018, the face of insurance actuarial services promises to change with the looming rise of '*micro-insurance*' based on risk assessment and management decisions sourced from the development of '*micro-actuarial tables*' produced by application of the models described above. These methods excel when applied to sparse data or datasets/samples derived from reduced (perhaps third party) sources.

Another project in 2017 produced a system to time large trades with the goal of minimizing market impact (since these bulk transactions may indicate a profitable external interest to vigilant outsiders). Of course, as often as this impact is undesirable, another scenario might benefit from this impact, so this predictive power presents a dual-opportunity that could not be presented without supervised machine learning and the application of advanced regression techniques reviewed herein.

SML in Retail

The retail industry provides many high-profile and highly visible success stories related to the rise of Artificial Intelligence. Once more, the common analytical factor is a presence of large, sociologically-derived datasets and the many profitable potentials associated with viable analysis of same. Indeed, retail operations present a predictive paradise with untold potential for discovery and advancement of these technologies.

Multiple studies and product releases in 2018, alone, pertain to this field of endeavors. Examples include use of supervised machine learning and linear regression modalities to the personalization of online marketing (big surprise there, Google!), stock and inventory management and optimization, logistics management and optimization, internal and external loss prevention, fraud detection, and many more. Due to the dynamic, highspeed, high-throughput nature of typical retail operations, SVMs also make a common appearance within this domain.

SML in the Travel/Entertainment Enterprise

Finally, though not exhaustively, the travel and entertainment enterprise present another massive source of sociological data demonstrating potential for vast returns on R&D investment as regards development of machine learning tools for commercial analyses. As of the time of this writing, SVMs as Kernel Machines appear commonly here to provide sentiment prediction for reviews and ratings, and personalized travel, as well as predictive pricing according to fluctuations in weather, socio-, politico- and economic phenomena.

Lesson Conclusion

Clearly, given the recent advent of Deep Learning technology, this review represents only the tip of the tip of the proverbial iceberg.   Countless problems await readymade solutions, and inestimable profits will accrue to those wise, intrepid few who dare venture forth in this huge technological arena to do battle with yesteryear's 'data demons'.   Wherever predictive requirements meet "big data", sparse/dense input, sparse/dense features and unknown composition, the methods described above will apply.   Thus far, this review has described a progression from smaller, simpler (and more restrictively constrained) datasets and solutions to modern graph-models and advanced regression methods that support analytical clarification of previously intractable problem domains.

Naturally, modern designers cannot accomplish these wonders within a purely theoretical framework.   This is a 'hands-on' business.   Accordingly, a brief code base review will further enlighten the interested student regarding the facility and efficacy of Deep Learning (Machine Learning) model development.

CODE BASE

Lesson Overview

For means of quick reference and convenience, the following sub-sections provide live-code samples intended to execute against live, downloadable datasets (where applicable). Perhaps, for most interested professionals, the 'big picture' presented below should seem... well, simple.

This is the creative power currently expressing itself via countless implementations of machine-learning solutions using a variety of deep learning software now available. The implementation – that is, the *syntactical* description and manipulation of even complex deep learning models should appear to be *easy*. In a manner of definition, this is certainly a true statement.

However, the development of practical deep learning solutions typically requires a bit more effort – most of it focused on manipulation of large datasets to make them presentable for ingestion and/or iterative refinement of model performance via repeated runs against multiple configurations and parameter settings (and more). This, then, might be the 'big picture' message presented below – software like Keras (and TensorFlow and Microsoft Cognitive Toolkit, *etc...*) make this process seem easy, although the final product will probably require greater application of art than science.

Keras Samples

Conveniently, *Keras* (at http://keras.io) includes a wide range of *Python*-based access to three popular deep learning software systems ('*back-ends*' – the software that provides functional implementation of Keras-directed models), TensorFlow and Microsoft Cognitive Toolkit. Even better, to support novice developers, this well-managed product presents a variety of fast, easy-to-learn tutorials ready for copy/paste into the *Integrated Development Environment* (*IDE*) of your choice – simply compile and run them at your convenience. Even better than better, to support live examination of code (and underlying back-end software) functionality, Keras provides multiple real-world datasets, which the developer may access with trivial effort.

Incidentally, the development process can be simply described, as well, although it can be, in practice, a rather complex undertaking. The code samples represent the command-line execution of key Keras features that relate to the preceding discussion. This is where development stops, at least within the context of this coursework. This is always where deployment begins.

At the end of the developmental process, Keras (via its underlying back-end software system) produces a trained 'model'. This is simply a file saved in the High-Density-File-5 (HDF5) format – this format, itself, presents a highly functional open-source API, which provides additional functionality to the highly-skilled developer. This model, then, may be installed and used within the production system as a stand-alone object (much like a word-processor application uses a variety of document file formats) via a number of methodologies. (Additionally, Keras supports output of JSON and YAML formats.) Again, a complete description of this development and deployment protocol exceeds the scope of this work.

Python

A word about Python follows. While a complete review of both Keras and the Python programming language exceeds the scope of this work, a few notes about essential concepts will be helpful. For those students familiar with programming methodologies, but unfamiliar with Python, the chief syntactical difference is Python's limited use of control characters – everything within these scripts is, for the most part, whitespace delimited. For example, indentation (the number of leading spaces or tabs) provides most code-block delimiting (except where the line ends in a 'comma' character, indicating a continuing list of parameters feeding a callable function – and even then, leading whitespace should be maintained as presented within the code below).

Finally, within most developmental languages, the comment character (in the case of Python, the '#' symbol) represents remarks provided by the developer to enhance coherence of a code-base. The following samples have internal comments from the originating demo, but they also contain remarks to support this discussion.

Loss Functions in Keras

Within Keras, model construction initiates with the 'compile' instruction, which accepts two arguments. One of these is a loss function, and the other is an optimizer. As previously described, a loss function is method for applying a '*penalty*' to the nodes of a graph model (or the parameters of a linear model) during '*training*', hence its crucial contribution to the definition of a model. Accordingly, Keras offers a variety of these tools to support development of flexible machine learning systems.

Mean-Based Methods

The vigilant student will note many familiar concepts in the code below. For example, the '*mean_squared_error loss function*', '*mean_absolute_error loss function*', '*mean_absolute_percentage_error loss function*' and '*mean_squared_logarithmic_error loss function*' all present easily discernible names that readily convey their functionality – many are described in the preceding text.

Other Methods

The '*hinge loss function*' (Appendix: Figure 1, Part A) presents a distribution (waveform) with a linear descent from the upper-left quadrant through the origin to one, where it plateaus at zero. The '*squared_hinge loss function*' (Appendix: Figure 1, Part B) represents the left (negative) side of the '*squared loss function*', which plots as a hyperbolic curve minimizing at 0, 1 – thus, the '*squared_hinge loss function*' is just the descending side of this curve. The '*logcosh loss function*' (Appendix: Figure 1, Part C) presents a shallow, positive hyperbole minimized at the origin. With the exception of the '*poisson loss function*'

(Appendix: Figure 1, Part E) (ordinarily, 'Poisson' is a proper noun), which plots as a 'normal-like' curve heavily distributed to the left, the remainder of the loss functions listed below generally describe a softly curving line with a vertical asymptote on the vertical axis and a horizontal asymptote at the horizontal axis. To be clear about these conformations, the diligent student will review Appendix A, Figure 1 and briefly examine examples online.

Code Samples

```
                        Loss Functions in Keras
###################  Loss function: mean_squared_error
keras.losses.mean_squared_error(y_true, y_pred)

###################  Loss function: mean_absolute_error
keras.losses.mean_absolute_error(y_true, y_pred)

###################  Loss function: mean_absolute_percentage_error
keras.losses.mean_absolute_percentage_error(y_true, y_pred)

###################  Loss function: mean_squared_logarithmic_error
keras.losses.mean_squared_logarithmic_error(y_true, y_pred)

###################  Loss function: squared_hinge
keras.losses.squared_hinge(y_true, y_pred)

###################  Loss function: hinge
keras.losses.hinge(y_true, y_pred)

###################  Loss function: categorical_hinge
keras.losses.categorical_hinge(y_true, y_pred)

###################  Loss function: logcosh
keras.losses.logcosh(y_true, y_pred)

###################  Loss function: categorical_crossentropy
keras.losses.categorical_crossentropy(y_true, y_pred)

###################  Loss function: sparse_categorical_crossentropy
keras.losses.sparse_categorical_crossentropy(y_true, y_pred)

###################  Loss function: binary_crossentropy
```

Loss Functions in Keras
keras.losses.binary_crossentropy(y_true, y_pred) ################### Loss function: **kullback_leibler_divergence** keras.losses.kullback_leibler_divergence(y_true, y_pred) ################### Loss function: **poisson** keras.losses.poisson(y_true, y_pred) ################### Loss function: **cosine_proximity** keras.losses.cosine_proximity(y_true, y_pred)

Activation Functions in Keras

Within the context of this discussion, an activation function abstractly represents the rate of '*action potential*' firing within a biological neuron. Within the graphs (matrices of nodes-and-edges, a network) of an '*Artificial Neural Network*' (*ANN*), the activation function defines the output of a given node, given a set of inputs; this output, in turn, serves as the next node's (or set of nodes) input. At its simplest, an action potential is a binary construct, in that it is either 'on' or 'off' (1 or 0), but nonlinear activation functions considerably enhance the capabilities of an ANN. Indeed, Keras supports a wide array of activation functions (to include advanced activations, which are not covered herein), each intended to support specific (or general) needs. The student will benefit from a brief review of these tools, which will include a number of recognizable concepts described above.

softmax

The '*softmax activation function*' ('*normalized exponential activation function*') (Appendix, Figure 1, Part M), generalizes a logistic function to 'flatten' an n-dimensional vector (array, list) of real values to a vector of the same size, in which each entry is in the range (0, 1) and all entries sum to 1 – a form of '*data normalization*'. When applied to categorical problems, the output of the softmax function represents a categorical distribution of probability distributed over 'n' possible outcomes (*e.g.*, a vocabulary of words to quantify the probability of the next word in a phrase or sentence). The waveform (or plotted curve) of softmax mirrors that of the sigmoid implementation, in that both demonstrate exponential tendencies, with the softmax sloping upward sharply at the end of the distribution and the sigmoid curve sloping sharply upward at the beginning of the distribution.

The 'softsign activation function' produces an 'S-shaped' curve with upper and lower asymptotes, while the 'softplus activation function' (Appendix, Figure 1, Part L) produces an intermediate curve that takes the form of the softmax, as attenuated toward the ReLu curve (which is a flat line to the vertical axis and then a linear slope through the upper right quadrant).

elu, selu, relu

The 'elu rectifier function', 'selu rectifier function', and 'relu rectifier function' are 'rectifiers' (Appendix, Figure 1, Part F & G). Within the context of machine learning and neural networks, a 'rectifier' is simply an activation function defined as the positive part of its argument (*i.e.,* the part in the upper-right quadrant – it remains 'zero' up to the vertical axis).

The 'rectified linear unit' (*ReLu* or *relu*) (Appendix A, Figure 1, Part F) plots as a straight, flat line that follows the horizontal axis to the origin, where it slopes directly upward into the top-right (positive) quadrant. The 'exponential linear unit' (*elu*) presents a smoothly ascending curve that approaches the origin from the negative (lower-left) quadrant of the plot, after which it presents a 'relu-like' linear plot that extends upward into the top-right quadrant. Finally, the 'selu function' ('scaled exponential linear unit') (Appendix A, Figure 1, Part G) presents a blend of the two, such that the resultant plot takes the general form of the ReLu with a smooth transition across the origin, like that of the elu function.

sigmoid and hard-sigmoid

The '*sigmoid activation function*' (Appendix A, Figure 1, Part H) presents a smooth, 'S-shaped' curve with upper and lower asymptotes and a relatively flat transition through the origin. The '*hard_sigmoid activation function*' (Appendix A, Figure 1, Part I) produces a simpler line, albeit with much steeper slopes that 'plateau' (or 'de-plateau') relatively quickly into the upper-right quadrant. Related, the '*tanh activation function*' ('*hyperbolic tangent activation function*') (Appendix A, Figure 1, Part J) produces a curve that resembles a 'flattened' sigmoid.

exponential

The '*exponential activation function*' ('*exponential [base e] activation function*') (Appendix A, Figure 1, Part N) produces a smooth curve with a lower asymptote on the horizontal axis and a gradual, though exponential, ascent into the upper-right quadrant. The slope begins increasing on the negative side of the vertical axis, such that the 'y-intercept' is typically positive and non-zero.

linear

The '*linear activation function*' ('*identity activation function*') (Appendix A, Figure 1, Part O) presents, as expected, a simple straight line passing through the origin into the positive quadrant. This function should not be confused with the linear rectifiers previously discussed – this is not a rectifier (which present a 'bent' line), since it plots with a single, non-bifurcated slope.

Code Samples

Activation Functions in Keras
#######################################

Activation Functions in Keras

```
# Softmax activation function: softmax
keras.activations.softmax(x, axis=-1)
########## Arguments
#  x: Input tensor.
#  axis: Integer, axis along which the softmax normalization is applied.
######   Return, Success Condition
#  Tensor, output of softmax transformation.
######   Return, Error Condition
#  ValueError: In case dim(x) == 1.


#######################################
#  Softplus activation function: softplus
keras.activations.softplus(x)
########## Arguments
#  x: Input tensor.
########## Returns
#  The softplus activation: log(exp(x) + 1).


#######################################
#  Softsign activation function: softsign
keras.activations.softsign(x)
########## Arguments
#  x: Input tensor.
########## Returns
#  The softplus activation: x / (abs(x) + 1).


#######################################
#  Exponential linear unit: elu
keras.activations.elu(x, alpha=1.0)
########## Arguments
#  x: Input tensor.
#  alpha: A scalar, slope of negative section.
########## Returns
#  The exponential linear activation: x if x > 0 and alpha * (exp(x)-1) if x < 0.


#######################################
#  Scaled Exponential Linear Unit (SELU): selu
keras.activations.selu(x)
########## Arguments
#  x: A tensor or variable to compute the activation function for.
########## Returns
#  The scaled exponential unit activation: scale * elu(x, alpha).
########## Note
#  To be used together with the initialization "lecun_normal".
#  To be used together with the dropout variant "AlphaDropout".
```

Activation Functions in Keras

```
#######################################
#  Rectified Linear Unit: relu
keras.activations.relu(x, alpha=0.0, max_value=None, threshold=0.0)
########## Arguments
#  x: Input tensor.
#  alpha: float. Slope of the negative part. Defaults to zero.
#  max_value: float. Saturation threshold.
#  threshold: float. Threshold value for thresholded activation.
########## Returns
#  A tensor.


#######################################
#  Hyperbolic tangent activation function: tanh
keras.activations.tanh(x)


#######################################
#  Sigmoid activation function: sigmoid
keras.activations.sigmoid(x)


#######################################
#  Hard sigmoid activation function: hard_sigmoid
keras.activations.hard_sigmoid(x)
########## Arguments
#  x: Input tensor.
########## Returns
#  Hard sigmoid activation:
#  0 if x < -2.5
#  1 if x > 2.5
#  0.2 * x + 0.5 if -2.5 <= x <= 2.5


#######################################
#  Exponential (base e) activation function: exponential
keras.activations.exponential(x)


#######################################
#  Linear (i.e. identity) activation function: linear
keras.activations.linear(x)
```

Optimizer Functions in Keras

In the context of this discussion, an *'optimizer'* is simply a function designed to ensure selection of optimal values within the network (typically, of node values, but this concept also applies to edge weights and a number of other related technological features). As might be expected, Keras supports a wide range of 'canned' routines to perform this service.

SGD

The *'sgd optimizer function'* (*Stochastic Gradient Descent*) (*SGD*) optimizer uses this system – the SGD system – to optimize coefficients. While a detailed review of SGD exceeds the scope of this course (read "Graph Models for Deep Learning"), the student will benefit from a brief summary, as follows. Essentially, SGD is a 'random walk' across a statistical landscape in search of optima (lowest-of-the-lows or highest-of-the-highs). Imagine a chaotic 2D waveform – that is, a wavy line drawn on a graph with multiple peaks and valleys in its distribution – and then imagine a series of similar lines stacked together to make a 3D "mountain range" of variations on this wave form. While true dimensions of a real distribution may be infinite, this 3D analogy adequately conveys the process. SGD randomly (stochastically) explores this landscape by picking a point in the terrain and then "wandering" around while sampling the local value and recording subsequent highs and lows. Repeating this process with a large number of "wanderers" will compile a list of highs and lows, or *'local optima'*. Selection of *'global optima'*, then, proceeds in a straightforward fashion by simply selecting the highest-of-highs or lowest-of-lows from the compiled discovery. This is, perhaps, one of the more common optimizers for complex Deep Learning (DL) models, and it additionally serves as a base for most of the optimizers described below.

Adagrad

The '*Adagrad optimizer function*' extends SGD by providing a '*per parameter learning rate*'. Essentially, Adagrad increases its learning rate for '*sparse parameters*', while decreasing its learning rate for '*non-sparse parameters*'. Here, the term '*sparse*' refers to the parameter's representation in the dataspace. Adagrad is common within natural language processing and image recognition analyses.

Adadelta

Keras' '*Adadelta optimizer function*' dynamically adapts its per-parameter learning rates over time using only first order information, a method for further optimizing computational performance. Adadelta requires no manual tuning and it remains robust to noisy gradients, model architecture selection, data modality variation and hyperparameter selection.

RMSprop

The '*RMSprop optimizer function*' ('*Root Mean Square Propagation*') is adaptive learning rate optimizer. RMSprop divides its learning rate for a parameter by calculating the average of magnitudes derived from previous parameter gradients.

Adam

The '*Adam optimizer function*' ('*Adaptive Moment Optimization*') combines the best features of Adagrad and RMSprop. This algorithm calculates an exponential moving average of the gradient (as with Adagrad) and the squared gradient (RMSprop) to calculate its parameter weights, providing a pair of input variables to control the influence of these affects (much as Elastic Net Regression combines Ridge Regression and Lasso Regression).

Adamax and Nadam and NAG

Related, the '*Adamax optimizer function*' benefits analytical systems demonstrating sparse parameter updates, reducing the model's susceptibility to gradient noise. The '*Nadam optimizer function*' combines Adam and '*Nesterov Accelerated Gradient*' (*NAG*) (a method that attempts to 'guide' the wanderer during gradient descent searches).

Code Samples

Optimizer Functions in Keras
#####################
Stochastic gradient descent optimizer: **SGD**
keras.optimizers.SGD(lr=0.01, momentum=0.0, decay=0.0, nesterov=False)
Includes support for momentum, learning rate decay, and Nesterov momentum.
########## Arguments
lr: float >= 0. Learning rate.
momentum: float >= 0. Parameter accelerates SGD in relevant direction, dampens oscillations.
decay: float >= 0. Learning rate decay over each update.
nesterov: boolean. Whether to apply Nesterov momentum.
#####################
RMSProp optimizer: **RMSprop**
keras.optimizers.RMSprop(lr=0.001, rho=0.9, epsilon=None, decay=0.0)
Default values recommended (except the learning rate, which can be freely tuned).
This optimizer is usually a good choice for recurrent neural networks.
########## Arguments

Optimizer Functions in Keras

```
###  lr: float >= 0. Learning rate.
###  rho: float >= 0.
###  epsilon: float >= 0. Fuzz factor. If None, defaults to K.epsilon().
###  decay: float >= 0. Learning rate decay over each update.


####################
###  Adagrad optimizer: Adagrad
keras.optimizers.Adagrad(lr=0.01, epsilon=None, decay=0.0)
###  Adagrad is an optimizer with parameter-specific learning rates
###  adapted relative to how frequently a parameter gets updated during training.
###  The more updates a parameter receives, the smaller the updates.
###  Default values recommended.
##########  Arguments
###  lr: float >= 0. Initial learning rate.
###  epsilon: float >= 0. If None, defaults to K.epsilon().
###  decay: float >= 0. Learning rate decay over each update.


####################
###  Adadelta optimizer: Adadelta
keras.optimizers.Adadelta(lr=1.0, rho=0.95, epsilon=None, decay=0.0)
###  Adadelta is a more robust extension of Adagrad that adapts learning rates
###  based on a moving window of gradient updates, instead of accumulating all
past gradients.
###  This way, Adadelta continues learning even when many updates have been
done.
###  Compared to Adagrad, in the original version of Adadelta you don't have to
set
###  initial learning rate. In this version, initial learning rate and decay factor can
be set.
###  Default values recommended.
##########  Arguments
###  lr: float >= 0. Initial learning rate, defaults to 1. It is recommended to leave it
at the default value.
###  rho: float >= 0. Adadelta decay factor, corresponding to fraction of gradient,
kept at each time step.
###  epsilon: float >= 0. Fuzz factor. If None, defaults to K.epsilon().
###  decay: float >= 0. Initial learning rate decay.


####################
###  Adam optimizer: Adam
keras.optimizers.Adam(lr=0.001, beta_1=0.9, beta_2=0.999, epsilon=None,
decay=0.0, amsgrad=False)
###  Default parameters follow those provided in the original paper.
##########  Arguments
###  lr: float >= 0. Learning rate.
###  beta_1: float, 0 < beta < 1. Generally close to 1.
```

Optimizer Functions in Keras

beta_2: float, 0 < beta < 1. Generally close to 1.
epsilon: float >= 0. Fuzz factor. If None, defaults to K.epsilon().
decay: float >= 0. Learning rate decay over each update.
amsgrad: boolean. Whether to apply the AMSGrad variant of this algorithm.

####################
Adamax optimizer: **Adamax**
keras.optimizers.Adamax(lr=0.002, beta_1=0.9, beta_2=0.999, epsilon=None, decay=0.0)
It is a variant of Adam based on the infinity norm.
Default parameters recommended.
######### Arguments
lr: float >= 0. Learning rate.
beta_1/beta_2: floats, 0 < beta < 1. Generally close to 1.
epsilon: float >= 0. Fuzz factor. If None, defaults to K.epsilon().
decay: float >= 0. Learning rate decay over each update.

####################
Nesterov Adam optimizer: **Nadam**
keras.optimizers.Nadam(lr=0.002, beta_1=0.9, beta_2=0.999, epsilon=None, schedule_decay=0.004)
Nadam is Adam RMSprop with Nesterov momentum.
Default values recommended.
######### Arguments
lr: float >= 0. Learning rate.
beta_1/beta_2: floats, 0 < beta < 1. Generally close to 1.
epsilon: float >= 0. Fuzz factor. If None, defaults to K.epsilon().

Initializer Functions in Keras

The base initializer function is imaginatively labeled '*initializer*'. Its functionality provides the base functionality of the methods that extend it, as described below. For the most part, the Keras function label adequately explains these operators, since the goal of an initializer is to '*initialize*' – or set the initial values of – an algorithmic system.

Zeros, Ones and Constant

For example, the '*Zeros initializer function*', '*Ones initializer function*' and '*Constant initializer function*' respectively initialize analytical coefficients to values of zero, one and a designer-defined constant.

VarianceScaling, Orthogonal and Identity

The '*VarianceScaling initializer function*' adapts its scale to the shape of weights, as derived from the underlying model architecture, while the '*Orthogonal initializer function*' generates a random matrix of initialization values. Again, as the label indicates, the '*Identity initializer function*' initializes across the identities of a matrix (diagonals), repeating where dimensions of the 2D graph are incongruous.

Uniform- and Normal-Distribution Initializers

Keras also provides a series of uniform initializers. The '*RandomUniform initializer function*', '*lecun_uniform initializer function*', '*glorot_uniform initializer function*' and '*he_uniform initializer function*' drawl their samples from a series of uniform, pre-limited distributions. Finally, its collection of normal initializers include the '*he_normal initializer function*', '*lecun_normal initializer function*', '*RandomNormal initializer function*', '*TruncatedNormal initializer function*' and '*glorot_normal initializer function*' perform a similar service using normal distributions.

Code Samples

Initializer Functions in Keras
###################

```
###################
###  Initializer Function: Initializer
keras.initializers.Initializer()
###  Initializer base class.


###################
###  Initializer Function: Zeros
keras.initializers.Zeros()
###  Initializer that generates tensors initialized to 0.


###################
###  Initializer Function: Ones
keras.initializers.Ones()
###  Initializer that generates tensors initialized to 1.


###################
###  Initializer Function: Constant
keras.initializers.Constant(value=0)
###  Initializer that generates tensors initialized to a constant value.
##########  Arguments
###  value: float; the value of the generator tensors.


###################
###  Initializer Function: RandomNormal
keras.initializers.RandomNormal(mean=0.0, stddev=0.05, seed=None)
###  Initializer that generates tensors with a normal distribution.
##########  Arguments
###  mean: a python scalar or a scalar tensor. Mean of the random values to
generate.
###  stddev: a python scalar or a scalar tensor. Std dev. of the random values to
generate.
###  seed: A Python integer. Used to seed the random generator.


###################
###  Initializer Function: RandomUniform
```

Initializer Functions in Keras

keras.initializers.RandomUniform(minval=-0.05, maxval=0.05, seed=None)
Initializer that generates tensors with a uniform distribution.
########## Arguments
minval: A python scalar or a scalar tensor. Lower bound of range of random values to generate.
maxval: A python scalar or a scalar tensor. Upper bound of range of random values to generate.
Defaults to 1 for float types.
seed: A Python integer. Used to seed the random generator.

####################
Initializer Function: **TruncatedNormal**
keras.initializers.TruncatedNormal(mean=0.0, stddev=0.05, seed=None)
Initializer that generates a truncated normal distribution.
These values are similar to values from a RandomNormal except that values more than two
standard deviations from the mean are discarded and re-drawn. This is the recommended
initializer for neural network weights and filters.
########## Arguments
mean: a python scalar or a scalar tensor. Mean of the random values to generate.
stddev: a python scalar or a scalar tensor. Standard deviation of the random values to generate.
seed: A Python integer. Used to seed the random generator.

####################
Initializer Function: **VarianceScaling**
keras.initializers.VarianceScaling(scale=1.0, mode='fan_in', distribution='normal', seed=None)
Initializer capable of adapting its scale to the shape of weights.
With distribution="normal", samples are drawn from a truncated normal distribution centered
on zero, with stddev = sqrt(scale / n) where n is:
number of input units in the weight tensor, if mode = "fan_in"
number of output units, if mode = "fan_out"
average of the numbers of input and output units, if mode = "fan_avg"
With distribution="uniform", samples are drawn from uniform distribution
within [-limit, limit], with limit = sqrt(3 * scale / n).
########## Arguments
scale: Scaling factor (positive float).
mode: One of "fan_in", "fan_out", "fan_avg".
distribution: Random distribution to use. One of "normal", "uniform".
seed: A Python integer. Used to seed the random generator.
########## Raises
ValueError: In case of an invalid value for the "scale", mode" or "distribution"

Initializer Functions in Keras

arguments.

```
####################
### Initializer Function: Orthogonal
keras.initializers.Orthogonal(gain=1.0, seed=None)
### Initializer that generates a random orthogonal matrix.
######### Arguments
### gain: Multiplicative factor to apply to the orthogonal matrix.
### seed: A Python integer. Used to seed the random generator.


####################
### Initializer Function: Identity
keras.initializers.Identity(gain=1.0)
### Initializer that generates the identity matrix.
### Only use for 2D matrices. If the long side of the matrix is a multiple of the
short side,
###   multiple identity matrices are concatenated along the long side.
######### Arguments
### gain: Multiplicative factor to apply to the identity matrix.


####################
### Initializer Function: lecun_uniform
keras.initializers.lecun_uniform(seed=None)
### LeCun uniform initializer.
### It draws samples from a uniform distribution within [-limit, limit] where limit
is
###   sqrt(3 / fan_in) where fan_in is the number of input units in the weight
tensor.
######### Arguments
### seed: A Python integer. Used to seed the random generator.
######### Returns
### An initializer.


####################
### Initializer Function: glorot_normal
keras.initializers.glorot_normal(seed=None)
### Glorot normal initializer, also called Xavier normal initializer.
### It draws samples from a truncated normal distribution centered
###   on 0 with stddev = sqrt(2 / (fan_in + fan_out)) where fan_in is the number of
input units
###   in the weight tensor and fan_out is the number of output units in the weight
tensor.
######### Arguments
### seed: A Python integer. Used to seed the random generator.
######### Returns
### An initializer.
```

Initializer Functions in Keras

```
####################
###  Initializer Function: glorot_uniform
keras.initializers.glorot_uniform(seed=None)
###  Glorot uniform initializer, also called Xavier uniform initializer.
###  It draws samples from a uniform distribution within [-limit, limit] where limit
is
###   sqrt(6 / (fan_in + fan_out)) where fan_in is the number of input units in the
weight tensor
###   and fan_out is the number of output units in the weight tensor.
##########  Arguments
###  seed: A Python integer. Used to seed the random generator.
##########  Returns
###  An initializer.


####################
###  Initializer Function: he_normal
keras.initializers.he_normal(seed=None)
###  He normal initializer.
###  It draws samples from a truncated normal distribution centered on 0 with
###   stddev = sqrt(2 / fan_in) where fan_in is the number of input units in the
weight tensor.
##########  Arguments
###  seed: A Python integer. Used to seed the random generator.
##########  Returns
###  An initializer.


####################
###  Initializer Function: lecun_normal
keras.initializers.lecun_normal(seed=None)
###  LeCun normal initializer.
###  It draws samples from a truncated normal distribution centered on 0
###   with stddev = sqrt(1 / fan_in) where fan_in is the number of input units in the
weight tensor.
##########  Arguments
###  seed: A Python integer. Used to seed the random generator.
##########  Returns
###  An initializer.


####################
###  Initializer Function: he_uniform
keras.initializers.he_uniform(seed=None)
###  He uniform variance scaling initializer.
###  It draws samples from a uniform distribution within [-limit, limit] where limit
###   is sqrt(6 / fan_in) where fan_in is the number of input units in the weight
tensor.
```

Initializer Functions in Keras
########## Arguments
seed: A Python integer. Used to seed the random generator.
########## Returns
An initializer.

COURSE CONCLUSION

Course Conclusion

Course Review

Since the belabored student has already reviewed the linear and non-linear regression methods described above, and is by now well aware of their applications within the realm of supervised machine learning problems, this conclusion will not excessively belabor points already established. Instead, as with all things human, these passages end with a word of hope and encouragement, followed by the inevitable caution.

Ideally, at the least, given progress of the 'plot' presented within this course, the student will now possess a minimal awareness of the past, have a firm grip on the present, and will, thus, be better prepared to anticipate the future of supervised learning with linear regression. Given the looming promise of quantum computing, which is uniquely suited to application of vast and complex artificial neural networks, these concepts will rapidly involve into something altogether unprecedented in the history of human civilization.

These are, indeed, promising times and this is a technology with vast, untapped potential. Before we wax smug, however, a word about free lunches (there are none).

"No Free Lunch"

The student who recalls the so-called 'Y2K Crisis', the 'Dot Com Bubble', the 'Housing Bubble', *et cetera*, will no doubt possess a well-honed 'hype-sensor'. Machine learning, artificial intelligence and deep learning (among a few coins of the concept), all present the enormous potential described above. 'Hot words' and hype abound. Truth may seem obscure.

In fact, deep learning technology will undoubtedly change the world – for better *and* worse. It will not replace *everything*. It will not solve *all* problems.

A current discussion in this regard assumes the 'edgelord-worthy' moniker, *"The No Free Lunch Theorems of Optimization"*, which dates to the mid-nineties and early investigations of advanced graph models and machine learning theory. The authors demonstrate an interesting conundrum then (and perhaps now) associated with the optimization of... stuff. In the case of machine learning, they postulate that the amount of labor invested in selecting an efficacious machine learning system might not, in fact (and in the long-term), provide much savings over development of more traditional, rule-based methods. *I.e.,* one set of methods is as likely to produce similar outcomes as any other.

To some extent, this is certainly true. Perhaps things will change in the near future to render the point moot.

Addressing this issue, the student might review state of the art programming methodologies for microcomputers (the PC, mostly), circa 1990. Then, memory measured in megabytes (if one could afford such extravagance), CPUs clocked in megahertz, and the new 'object-oriented' programming languages benefited enormously from tightly controlled production methods and relentless optimizations. Ten years later, systems became sufficiently powerful to negate the need for such diligence (practically, if not professionally) and optimization efforts turned elsewhere.

Quantum computing, however it arises, will change the face of this technology, perhaps more profoundly than adaption of GPUs has more recently impacted contemporary systems. Optimization interests will again change focus. Powerful and sprawling networks will likely become the norm. Or not.

This being the case, however, a wise developer will probably *not* use an RBF Kernel to categorize text. Why?

A Closing Analogy

If 'Deep Learning' represents an apex of the modern machine learning corpus, then the models discussed above must represent finger-tip contact with the analytical world of its applications. The models described above provide increasingly adaptable and sensitive solutions to large, sparse, chaotic data sources, which abound in the natural world. Innumerable examples await exploration.

From a ground-level perspective of this technological advance, a broad, rich terrain spreads endlessly into the future before the professionals engaged in its development. Fertile valleys and lucrative heights swell with low-hanging fruit. Go forth and prosper!

Course Conclusion

APPENDIX

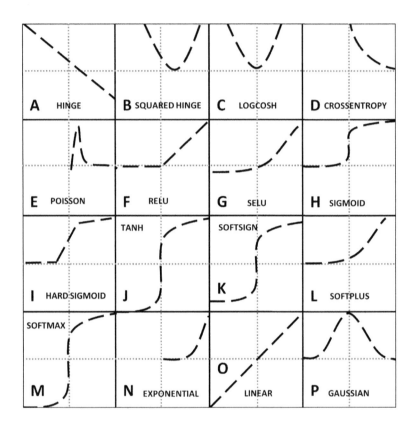

FIGURE 1

Glossary of Terms

END

ABOUT THE AUTHOR

Born in Texas and currently residing in Washington D.C., Stephen Donald Huff is an author of fiction novels, short stories and poetry. He is also a published scientist with expertise in bioinformatics (computational biology) and machine learning. Message him at Stephen@StephenHuff.com.

Printed in Great Britain
by Amazon

47278456R00091